DEBT and
CIRCUSES

Protecting Business Owners from
their Enemies, their Allies, and Themselves

CLAY M. WESTBROOK

Debt and Circuses

Contents

Dedication

This book is dedicated to
Jack Alfred Miller (1946-2013) and his family.

Rest in Peace.

Part 1

"Never despair, but if you do, work on in despair."

–Edmund Burke

Introduction

i.

This book is an attempt to explain what you should know, and what we learned, from seven years of loan workouts, lawsuits, and bankruptcies during the Great Recession. This is not an autobiography; while the events recalled are true, my role varied in each case from lead negotiator, to researcher, to brain-stormer, or merely an Observer of Interesting Things. The outcomes resulted from the efforts of many talented people (the "we" used through this book) including finance and accounting advisors, lawyers, and courageous entrepreneurs who followed the counterintuitive, asymmetrical, and risky advice of a few creative consultants.

If you read no further or learn nothing else, the point of this book is as follows: the outcome of a dispute, or the solution to a financial problem, doesn't have to be the way the creditors explain it, nor does it have to be the way *your* lawyer, accountant, financial advisor, or anyone else explains it. The way disputes work in reality isn't written in textbooks or newspaper articles, or taught in seminars or executive MBA classes, or explained from a comfortable leather chair in a law office.

Forget about doing the right thing, forget about the legal merits, and forget about logic. This principle also applies to most other lawsuits and almost all partnership divorces (business *or* personal). Solutions come from psychology and math, human nature, and realizing neither side understands (nor cares) what the other side is saying.

Business owners, chief financial officers, accounting and finance professionals, risk-non-averse attorneys (to the extent such beings exist), and Observers of Interesting Things will learn how to protect themselves, their clients, and others in restructuring and litigation/bankruptcy cases. Whatever you may learn, give the credit to those courageous clients and talented advisors, and the entertaining, if not ridiculous, stranger-than-fiction situations in which these people found themselves.

By showing you what talented advisors accomplished, hopefully you will have the confidence to trust your instincts, never forget to account for human nature when evaluating the options, and become the person on the team who can see where the borrower, the lawyers, or other advisors may be falling into a trap.

ii.

Just because everyone thinks they know the outcome does not mean the game isn't worth playing. The political science eggheads on TV gave Hillary Clinton a 99% chance of beating Bernie Sanders in the 2016 Michigan Democratic Primary. She lost. How many situations can you think of in history where *everybody* said that because of the laws, or the rules of the game, or one side's overwhelming power, the outcome would *never* be in doubt, and everybody was wrong? How does it happen?

It happens because people can do extraordinary things when it's *their* life, family, livelihood, clients, or teammates on the line. But first you have to understand yourself and your situation, find the courage to do what must be done, and step into the arena. Going through the process doesn't necessarily mean playing by the rules. The way the system is designed, playing by the rules means certain defeat.

When people learn that I work with businesses and advisors negotiating loan workouts and financial restructuring plans, they usually respond with, "Wow, I know some people who sure could've used your help," or "I wish we had met three years ago," or a variation thereof. They tell woeful stories about totally uncooperative creditors, cowardly lawyers, failed businesses, bankruptcy, bad real estate deals, divorces, downsized lifestyles, even moving back in with parents.

Many people in this arena aspired to write a book about it, myself included. Talking about it and actually doing it... well, you know. Writing a book is a big undertaking, which requires inspiration. That inspiration came from a young woman's very different story.

Chapter 1

"They said it wasn't an option."

I met Maria in 2015. Five years earlier, she had moved from California to Georgia with her husband, Gary, and two children. Her husband's real estate business never recovered from the aftermath of the Financial Crisis of 2008-09, and their experiences with creditors destroyed her whole world. Her marriage was over, her son dropped out of college, and she and her daughter were working on a new life.

I wanted to hear Maria's story, so we met one afternoon.

"The mortgage company told us that we weren't allowed to file for bankruptcy. They said it wasn't an option," Maria explained.

She didn't realize what this meant. The mortgage company didn't just lie to them; they violated state and federal laws in doing so. We might have had a case, or at least an issue to run with, which is usually enough. But it was too late.

"I just remember the phone never stopped ringing. Collections people. I still have anxiety whenever the phone rings."

Three years later, the tension lingered on. I ordered another drink. The bartender was happy to have something to do; the dinner crowd wouldn't arrive for hours.

"And you never talked to a lawyer?"

By this point, the question was rhetorical.

"*No, Gary thought it would be a waste of time, and we didn't have money. He didn't see why we should give money to a lawyer when nothing could be done. He owed the money, so it'd make no difference.*"

Her husband's depression debilitated him to the point that she could no longer justify his actions, or her own. After four long years of collections calls and fighting to survive, Maria decided that moving out was the least-bad option.

"And when did he kill himself?"

"*He killed himself three weeks after I moved out.*"

"Could I Borrow $2,000,000 for Six Hours?"

January, 2011.

The Client owns a retail business. He also has several other investments, which are largely other shopping centers and other real estate investments. The client makes all of the major decisions while a business partner runs sales and day-to-day operations. Looking at the financial statements of the company, we learn that the guarantor's partner collects a salary and is an investor in a competing company. The client makes the major decisions, but he doesn't make the decisions very well.

The retail company has a maturity default on a $3.5 million loan from a large national bank. They have made no progress trying to obtain a renewal or extension of the loan because the loan was originated by a small local bank, which was later acquired by the current lender, a larger bank. As strange as it may sound, the big banks make little effort to work with legacy customers of the banks they acquire; their motivation for these acquisitions is primarily the deposits and branch locations. The "assets," (i.e. the loans) don't seem as important.

The successor bank isn't interested in renewing the loan because they aren't interested in continuing the relationship. Another reason the client had no movement from the bank on renewing or modifying was because another family member had defaulted on a larger loan. Looking at the financials of the company, we learn that the business has negative cash flow and a large amount of accounts payable, which are also delinquent.

We look at the operational issues and find that the stores are in poor locations and poor condition. This is not surprising, because when the revenue of a business starts declining, maintenance expenses are among the first to go. Instead, the owner often funnels money into personal expenses—the country club membership, the vacation home(s), and financing the lifestyle of unemployed adult children. This case was no different.

Originally the game plan for this company was to acquire a large number of locations and sell out to one of the big public retailers. The large public retailers do not want to go through all of the unpleasantness of zoning approvals and don't have local people on the ground with the right relationships. Our clients know how to market their locations to these buyers, but with retail suffering greatly, the big guys will want rock bottom prices.

Meanwhile, our guarantor, who used to be very wealthy, has fallen on hard times. He had huge contingent liabilities in the form of other loan guarantees, and his cash position significantly eroded because he owns many properties encumbered by loans. He has to fund the debt payments from cash; the land isn't income-producing. The guarantor also has ownership interests in several startup companies, and to protect his ownership interest while the startups are losing money, he must fund the capital calls. The guarantor's cash is dwindling.

Smart business investors will tell you that assets are, at best, worthless until you sell them. Liquidity and positive cash flow are essential to any business. As discussed elsewhere, when liquidity of an asset dries up, be it mountain vacation home lots, collateralized debt obligations, or parachute pants, how do you determine what something's worth without positive cash flow? If nobody wants to buy a Member's Only jacket that people would pay $100 for last year, then today it's worth $0 if you can't sell it. Now, value may return, but that takes time and the assets value to the owner depends on the ability to cover the overhead costs between now and then.

The bank doesn't have time to wait. This loan must go. They do not want a relationship with this borrower, and they want this loan of their books. The lender is only interested in two outcomes: they want the loan paid off in full, or they want the guarantor to make a significant principal payment, which would use the last of his cash reserve, in exchange for a 12-month extension.

We eventually persuaded the lender to take 65 cents on the dollar in exchange for a full release of everything, i.e., the company kept the collateral.

The key to getting this deal settled was the nature of the real estate: all of the sites were not owned, but leased. Why does this matter? Because real estate is an asset, but lease payments are a liability. Whether the location has sales or not, the rent comes due. The company's occupancy was down, revenue was down, and lease payments on many of the locations were behind. It was a bad situation.

Our argument to the lender was that their collateral was worth less than zero, and that the guarantor did not have the cash or unencumbered assets to pay off the loan. Even if he did, he wouldn't have any cash left to carry all of his other investments, and would go broke. (This argument means nothing to lenders who don't have multiple loans with the same borrower/guarantor, but in rare cases it matters quite a bit.) If the bank took the collateral, they would be assuming the lease payments on all of the leased locations, as well as upkeep and deferred maintenance, and also have to run the business.

Also, whether the bank's security documents were done correctly was unclear. The originating bank was sloppy in their documentation of the loan and description of the collateral, and it's doubtful the acquiring lender ever knew or cared about the problems with the documentation when it bought the bank.

We walked through all of the guarantor's contingent liabilities with the asset manager[1] and the bank's legal counsel, providing them with trailing and

---

[1] The "asset manager" in all cases is the person or people the lender has employed who is responsible for resolving the case in question and is, with few exceptions, the sole point of contact with the lender. When the bank brings legal counsel into the case, their attorneys often serve as an additional point of contact to communicate to the lender or,

projected cash flow statements to show that the company is losing money, and the losses are accelerating. What would the bank's recovery be, net of legal fees, court costs, collections costs, and so forth?

We argued that by the time the bank filed a lawsuit against the guarantor and obtained a judgment, (assuming they could get a judgment), the guarantor would have nothing left to take. We prepared and provided to the asset manager a package of updated information and projections that demonstrated that the guarantor is unlikely to be solvent by the time the bank gets its judgment.

As noted elsewhere, a lawsuit is usually good news for the borrower. In our experience, if the borrower/defendant basically puts up no defense to the lawsuit and makes no attempt to delay, the fastest a plaintiff could obtain a judgment would be six to nine months. This assumes that the lender's attorney is aggressive and files for summary judgment as soon as possible, which rarely is the case. But the rule of thumb is: one month to answer the lawsuit, a six-month discovery period[2] (though it could be more, or a little less), one month to file summary judgment[3], then 30 days after summary judgment to appeal the court's ruling. This assumes we do not file a response to the summary judgment motion. We can file a response if (a) we have an issue or argument that would not be a violation of the lawyer's professional duty to not make frivolous claims AND (b) a lawyer who will make the argument. The court would rule on the motion an undeterminable time later, which in state court can be anywhere

with the occasional bank, may become the sole point of contact in the asset manager's stead.

[2] "Discovery Period' is a legal term of art. During this period all sides are entitled to send lists of questions (called 'interrogatories' or 'requests for admission'), all of which the other side must either answer under oath (in writing) or object to the court. There's also Requests for Production of Documents, and depositions, which aren't held in a courtroom but are still treated as courtroom testimony under oath. The purpose is for the plaintiff to establish the facts that prove the case and for the defendant to establish disputes of those facts.

[3] "Summary Judgment" means that the court rules that no trial on the merits is necessary. Either party may file a Motion for Summary Judgment, which argues (basically) that if the court considers all of the facts that neither party disputes, the judge should rule in their favor because the applicable law is clear. The other side then responds that essential factual disputes remain, and/or that the law is unclear or that a different law applies.

*between two months and never (but probably three to six months) and
in federal court the ruling may come a bit sooner.*

After our client reached a settlement with the lender, a funny thing
happened. A national retail chain sent the company a contract to purchase
half of the locations for an amount that could make the discounted payoff in
full with money to spare. With the additional proceeds, the company could
recapitalize the business, and the guarantor would have funds to keep the rest
of his investments going. Remember, the sale contract was not for all of the
locations. If the sale went through, the company would own the remaining
locations *free and clear.*

Our client, of course, wanted to make that sale, but also wanted to pay off
the bank at the agreed discount. To accomplish this feat, the current lender
and the national retail chain could not know of the other transaction. We had
two transactions we wanted to close, and the closings needed to be
simultaneous because the client had no money and needed the proceeds from
the purchase to pay off the lender. The only people who knew about both
transactions were the guarantor, their lawyers, and us. There were concerns
about the documents. How could we accomplish such a feat without making
material misrepresentations to the bank or the purchaser? We explored many
possibilities but never could settle on one that made everyone comfortable.

> *Oh, East is East, and West is West,*
> *and never the twain shall meet,*
>
> *Till Earth and Sky stand presently*
> *at God's great Judgment Seat;*

−Rudyard Kipling, The Ballad of East and West

We were stuck. The client needed $2 million to pay off the bank, which
could be paid back with the proceeds of the sale transaction when it closed.
The client needed to borrow $2 million for a day or two.

Who are you going to call when you need to borrow $2 million for two
days? Enter the Hard Money Lender.

Now, hard money lenders love making money, and the only thing more important to them than making money is *not losing money.* The risk was that the Hard Money Lender ("HML") wasn't 100 percent sure that the purchaser would close and pay his loan in two days. If he couldn't, then what? The HML had to underwrite the loan as if he would be the permanent lender. In other words, he needed to loan the money to pay off the bank, but would have to wait until the borrower could pay back the loan, if ever.

Nobody told the bank about the sale of assets to the ultimate purchaser. The bank never asked what would happen to the collateral. What they wanted to know was the source of the funds. The borrower told the truth: it was a third-party loan that would buy the bank's loan and modify it according to the terms to which the guarantor and HML had agreed. The HML's legal counsel negotiated the terms of the sale of the bank's loan to the new lender for the agreed discounted payoff. The bank understood that there was to be a renegotiation/modification between the new lender and the borrower after the sale of the loan.

The loan purchase transaction closed, and a few hours later the sale to the national chain closed, and the company paid off the hard money loan, the company now owned the remaining locations free and clear, and had cash to fund operations.

The hard money lender made a six-figure fee and an unimaginable return on the investment, and the money never really was at risk. The buyer of the assets was ready, they had negotiated all documents, due diligence was finished, and all that was left was to sign documents and fund. It takes money to make money.

The fee was exorbitant, but for the company well worth it. They wiped off $3 million from their balance sheet, owned half the assets free and clear, and had cash to fund operations. Life was good.

· · · · ·

Are the ethical, professional and legal gears of your mind grinding to a halt over the conclusion of this deal? The outcome was the best outcome for all of the parties, and the sleight of hand required to get the deal done was essential. If either the bank or the purchasing company discovered the other transaction, both would have killed the deal. And even if they didn't kill the deal at that point, the borrower would have to kill it himself.

Why would the borrower kill the deal? Yes, even if the borrower paid all of the sale proceeds to the bank, the borrower would still have the other half of the locations free and clear. But why would the borrower do that deal? If all of the sales proceeds went to the lender, the company would be stuck with a pile of lease obligations and no cash for operations. The company would quickly go out of business.

In that case, the borrower would have no reason to sell. Even if the borrower walked away from the deal, the borrower and guarantor still had cash reserves to fund legal maneuvering against the bank's collections efforts. If the only other option is going out of business, fighting on makes more sense as long as you have bullets. And in this war, the bullets are available cash.

If the bank had discovered the potential buyer and the contemplated transaction, could the bank force the borrower to do the deal? No, because only the borrower can sell, and all the lender can do is prevent the sale, not force the borrower to perform. The bank does not, nor did they ever, own the collateral. They could not sell the collateral without first foreclosing, which they certainly did not wish to do.

Why would the purchaser kill the deal? Greed, of course. The purchaser only looked at the assets, not the overall company. The buyer knew the borrower was in financial trouble because they were selling the assets at a bargain price, but the buyer didn't know the extent of the financial distress. The buyer thought all of the proceeds were going to the bank. If the buyer knew the bank would take less to release the assets, they would've demanded a lower price from the seller because they didn't know the seller desperately needed the excess cash to keep going. Unquestionably, the buyer would've tried to re-trade the deal if they learned of the bank's discounted payoff.

Even more likely, the buyer would have walked away from the deal entirely, thinking they could buy the assets for that lower price after the bank foreclosed. "Why should we pay $3 million today for something we can buy for $2 million after the bank takes it?" Although this is surely not the case, this would be the thought process. The client would have to convince them that their thought process was wrong, and this would be almost impossible because the buyer was a big S&P 500 public company. They could have waited forever for what they perceived to be the better deal.

The problem for the buyer was that waiting to buy from the bank wouldn't take into account the practical difficulties the bank would have in even getting their hands on the assets in the first place, particularly the tenacity of this particular client. Nor did it consider bank regulatory requirements that require appraisals, marketing periods, etc., for the sale of bank-owned assets. Sure, stories abound of back room, off market, sweetheart deals between banks and buyers looking to get their hands on a borrower's property. But that's easier said than done, and the purchaser was also a public company, which would have complicated matters considerably.

Why would the bank have killed the deal if they found out about the sale of the assets? Several reasons come to mind.

The bank would be thinking how they could explain the transaction to the committee or the regulators who will review the loan file. Saying, "We lost $6 on this bad loan," is easier than saying, "We only lost $3 on this bad loan, but the borrower put $3 in his pocket."

What? Why didn't you get the borrower's $3, too? What if news of this gets in the papers?

The lender considers the borrower keeping any money from the purchase as taking money that belongs to the bank.

If he can sell a widget for $10, and you can only sell the widget for $4, is he stealing $6 from you?

In the eyes of the bank, yes. But of course in reality, the borrower isn't taking anything from the lender when a deal funds a discounted payoff that is higher than the bank's likely recovery.

The borrower keeping the remaining locations after the discounted payoff would be a non-starter. The bank would have NEVER released them if they learned of the purchase. Instead, the bank would have insisted that the borrower hand over the other locations as part of the deal, or at least would've kept their security interest in place.

You might be thinking, "Well, the bank can just go cut a deal with the retail company to sell the assets after they foreclose." This sounds simple but ignores important practical considerations.

- First, *just foreclosing* on dozens and dozens of retail locations, some owned, some leased, in multiple states and counties, would be a hugely time-consuming and expensive endeavor, even if the borrower did not contest the foreclosures, which this borrower surely would (there is also the issue of foreclosing and inheriting a liability discussed above).

    o The lender probably didn't have all of the deeds and leases in its possession. Nor had anyone read and understood the terms of what documentation they did have.

    o If landlord estoppels existed, in which the landlord agrees to honor the lease if the lender forecloses on the tenant's leasehold interest, do we have all of them? What do they say? If none existed, the lender would have to negotiate a consent with the owner, and if they did exist, the lender is still going to want an acknowledgement from the landlord, which also will be negotiated.

- Bankers are in the banking business, not the retail real estate business. A bank won't have the sophistication to negotiate such a transaction with a major retail company. Once the assets become "bank-owned," a new set of regulations come into play regarding the liquidation, and will likely result in either listing the locations one by one, which requires excess time and money, or a simple auction of everything, in which the bank would likely get less than the $2.2 million they received.

- Third, and most important, is Lender Liability. Bankers are risk averse—what if the bank tried to cut a deal with the retail company and not only failed, but caused their borrower's deal to crater?

Answer: the bank doesn't get paid and is getting sued by its borrower.

The other pieces of the transaction shouldn't matter, but they do. Why? Politics and optics. It doesn't *look good* for the bank to leave the borrower standing. Critics won't listen to the reasoning because of their preconceived narrative and the bank's inability to clearly explain and understand the transaction.

Despite all of our reasoning, most bankers would only be focused on their bank getting less than the borrower owed, and the borrower keeping a portion of the sale proceeds, and particularly keeping a portion of the collateral, would be totally unacceptable. This is true even when the bank's recovery is greater than it otherwise would be.

Although convoluted and complex legally and financially, and involving millions of dollars, this story is a basic overview of the thinking that goes into achieving a settlement of a commercial loan. The process unfolds in basically the same sequence, and it doesn't matter if the dispute involves an $80 million working capital line of credit for the largest employer in the town and the six surrounding counties, or an $80 thousand loan on a worthless residential lot five miles from the beach that the developer's real estate listings described as "steps from the Gulf of Mexico."

The process is the same. What is different is the people, those peoples' egos and motivations, and 10,000 different facts and circumstances.

* * * * *

Maria wanted to beat the evening rush hour, so we called it a day.

"The final few days were different," she explained. *"Our daughter stayed in regular contact with him and told me that he seemed to be doing better."*

"He had made up his mind and was at peace with his decision," I blurted out like a 5th grader, too eager to show that I knew the answer.

Oftentimes when suicidal people resolve themselves to committing the act, they may be relieved or even cheerful. Men in particular will throw themselves into planning their own death; ending their life becomes their life's purpose, thinking, "This time, finally, I will succeed at something." Maria's husband was feeling better because his problems were solved. He would rid himself of his debt problems and his marital problems, permanently.

"And despite a suicide, the life insurance still paid out?"

"Fortunately, yes. I paid off all of the creditors and still had a small nest egg left for the kids."

"And you even paid off the ones you weren't legally obligated to pay?"

"That's right. I paid them all back." She said proudly.

This upset me. To the creditors, she wasn't a young mother with three jobs and a dead husband. They didn't care that her son was failing out of college because of the stress surrounding the situation, or that her daughter came home to find a policeman in the driveway, there to tell her that her missing dad had been found—in the barn, dead by his own hand. Those bills could've been negotiated down or out, and the extra money could have gone into that nest egg.

In the grand scheme, by that point Maria had no fight left in her. She was showing up every day for life, working hard, and moving on. I was still mad. I walked back to the office, fuming.

All they hear is "there isn't any point, you are sure to lose, don't waste the time and money." These people should realize that it doesn't necessarily have to be that way.

Instead, suicide. My God. I never even met the man, yet I still feel the anger and guilt. 'How could that son of a bitch do that? If only we had known; we could've done something."

We all said 'I should write a book about everything that happened.' Nobody ever did.

Chapter 2

"Last time I paid."

A dedication, of sorts.

One of the worst aspects of advising financially stressed business owners has been meeting with prospective clients when it's too late. We want to take on a case, achieve good results, have a little fun along the way, and make money. Far too often, however, the advice to the borrower was to file for personal bankruptcy. Not enough cash was left on hand because of borrowing more and more to try to keep all of the creditors at bay, while at the same time trying to keep everyone happy on the home front, and wasting money by trying to keep up appearances or staying in denial.

A mutual business contact introduced me to Maria and thought she was well-suited to assist me with several projects. I called her and introduced myself, explained my consulting firm, and what I needed. We met a few weeks later to review a proposal, and Maria told me she had a particular interest in my line of work.

"I wish we had known about you three years ago. My husband could have used your help."

If people don't say, "I bet you've been busy," they say, "I wish we had met a few years ago," like saying to a car salesman "Oh, you sell Buicks? That's so cool. I *just bought* a Buick the other day." Nevertheless, the stories do interest me, hearing different stories of people in similar situations doing the same thing and getting the same outcome.

"Oh wow, what happened? Did he have to file for bankruptcy?"

"No, he killed himself in 2012."

The greatest purpose here is to save one person, who we will never know, who was close to that edge, that point of no return, and received the right piece of advice or encouragement and decided to fight on another day. And the next day, decided to give it another go. Then made it through the next day and eventually recovered and survived to tell their story. *"You have no idea how close I was to doing something crazy."*

This book is dedicated to that person.

The life of business owners and managers in the new economy.

The vast majority of business owners or managers never put a dime in their pocket that they didn't earn themselves. In the twentieth century, people worked, saved, retired, and never asked for help, while at the same time they were always willing to lend a helping hand. Parents put their kids through college, and when they graduated sent them on their way. Entrepreneurs worked with a passion for their business and aspired to a comfortable retirement and passing wealth on to the next generation.

As the 20th century became the 21st, many people played by the same rules and were ruined in the Financial Crisis and Great Recession. Honest people lost their savings and/or livelihood and had to start all over, many of them late in life. Facing up to and confronting these challenges is more difficult than becoming a martyr, withdrawing from your social circles, downsizing your life, and casting the blame elsewhere.

This is not to say that the other side is not honorable. Large institutions such as banks or government agencies are intimidating, but they are run by *people.* These large institutions are managed by folks who have families and aspirations, vulnerabilities and weaknesses, like you. And, like you, they have a job to do, and an often difficult and thankless job at that.

The difference is that the rules and resources are stacked heavily in their favor.

Inside the Mind of a Borrower in Trouble

Since the Financial Crisis and Great Recession, most businesses are walking a tightrope in this economy, and one unexpected gust of wind from an unexpected direction can put a person's job, career, or business in jeopardy.

Emotionally charged, contentious disputes with large bureaucratic institutions and/or business partners are different from normal business disputes or transactions. Sure, both sides are angry at one another and suspect the motivations and truth of the statements of the other side. But debtor/creditor disputes and partnership breakups are closer to divorce cases than business negotiations.

Emotions run high. The emotional investment in these deals is amazing. After a hundred or so cases, we learned that most screaming and accusing was an act, an intimidation tactic. Still, they don't have to put on much of an act—they are furious, envious at times, and have zero trust in anything we say or our clients say. That's a smart move on their part in these situations, and we have to break through that mindset.

Divorce lawyers share the same experiences—they say that in divorce cases, both sides accuse the other of lying, cheating and stealing, and usually both are correct. Divorce lawyers generally mistrust their own clients. Workouts and restructuring aren't much different. We expect the client to give us only the parts of the story they think will help, and choose to conceal facts and circumstances they think will hurt.

Every engagement begins with a difficult process of convincing a client that they have to tell us the truth, and that we are going to tell their lenders the truth (presented carefully), and their lenders aren't going to believe us for a long, long time—if ever. The client's assumptions are often wrong about whether a given piece of information is harmful or helpful. That which the creditor might perceive as helpful to their case, or an accessible source of repayment, is probably not helpful in reality.

After all, our clients are in default of obligations to the creditor, usually because of failing to pay but not always, or they are about to default. If the borrower had a valid source of repayment, he wouldn't be there, and if the borrower could pay but wants to try to run a game to get a special deal, we wouldn't take the case. Being a party to a potential fraud isn't appealing for some reason.

Furthermore, it won't work. If the borrower is legally obligated to pay, and has funds that are a secured and valid source of repayment, the borrower should pay, and the borrower will pay eventually. The only way around that is to commit fraud.

That being said, gray areas exist, as well as perfectly legal ways to protect assets, and we will, and should, use all of them where possible. Use the many clever ways to hide assets in plain sight, take advantage of the other side's lack of attention to detail, or demonstrate to the creditors that if they go after certain assets, it won't be worth the cost, and we will fight tooth and nail every step of the way. These types of situations are difficult to describe in the abstract, so we will go through several real cases showing how it can happen.

Unlike business transactions where either party can break off negotiations when the parties cannot agree, there is no walking away in these cases. Moreover, the other side has virtually unlimited resources, and the deck is stacked in their favor.

The most difficult aspect of these cases is managing the borrower's emotions and expectations. There is always a huge financial stake in the outcome. Keeping clients optimistic is difficult. We go through a process of educating the clients about their unknown strengths, the adversary's unknown weaknesses, and how threats can be opportunities. What may appear to be bad news at first blush will be good news in reality.

Part of our job is to help clients understand that strategies and the ultimate goals will change with the passage of time and as new information comes to light. We must convince and continue to reinforce with them that, yes, this will be over one day, and you will move on; however, you have to fight to avoid personal bankruptcy and protect your business and your family.

You have to fight. You have no other choice.

We can't always convince clients of this basic truth. More than a few decided to surrender for no other reason than they didn't have stomach for the fight, justifying the surrender on moral grounds about doing the honorable thing. We vehemently disagree that such a course is honorable. This is discussed later.

Sometimes a settlement may look bad by itself, but makes sense and fits in with the borrower's big picture and goals. In other cases, such as the retail company above, clients got the most ridiculous and amazing results imaginable, while the lender walked away thinking they had cleaned our clock.

When working with troubled businesses and debtor/creditor conflict, the result will not be one where either "the borrower won" or "the lender won." It is a process. The facts of each situation determine borrower strategy and the outcome. The "process" is educating the lender—because the lender can't do anything to put money in the borrower's pocket to pay. If you don't know your rights and have the right strategy, the creditor will do their job: take your cash until you don't have any, then take your property and your business anyway. This happens every day.

• • • • •

August, 2010

Randolph Everett had lost everything, but hadn't yet realized it. He was one of Atlanta's top developers and a household name in the Atlanta real estate community. Tom Wolfe's "Charlie Croker" character in his novel *A Man in Full* may have been partially drawn from the man. The man wasn't used to hearing bad news, and he certainly didn't expect anyone disagreeing with him.

All of his properties were collateral for various loans. As a builder and land man, he was used to running the same game in every recession and real estate downturn the Atlanta market threw at him—borrow huge sums from small community banks, which would need him more than he needed them. If the real estate market went south, the bank would work out a modification because if he failed, the bank could also fail.

When explaining how the rules have changed in presentations, we often tell his story of *last time I paid.* "Last time I paid," Randolph explained. You could tell he had given this speech on many prior occasions. "When the real estate market declined in the early 2000s, I paid. When the big real estate bust of the late 80s-early 90s wiped out many developers, I paid back every loan. The early 80s recession, the stagflation of the late 70s, the early 70s recession, despite all of these downturns, I paid back every dime I ever borrowed. And you tell me to quit paying these loans and not pay them back?"

Well tell us, Mr. Everett, in all of the downturns you describe, what did yourlenders do?

"We'd argue, maybe scream and holler at each other, but in the end, they did what made sense. They cut the interest rates, extended terms, advanced working capital to complete projects, or suspend principal payments. When the market rebounded, I'd get caught up on everything."

And now, this time, what are your lenders doing?

"Well, now that you mention it, they're raising my interest rates. The bank will only give short-term extensions, and they want huge principal payments for that. They've halted all construction advances, so I've had to lay off my people, and the half-finished houses are rotting on the lots. They aren't making any sense."

So what happens if you keep paying?

"I'll run out of cash in a few months."

Then, Mr. Everett, what will your lenders do?

. . . . .

We expect the same course of action in each case when we examine how a business, or a businessman, gets into financial trouble. The size, industry, or type of debts doesn't make much difference. Numbers are numbers, money is money, value is value, and we can all objectively determine this information.

However, a person's "objectivity" depends on many facets of the person's temperament, personality, and—most importantly—motivations.[4]

Never forget that when circumstances put people in these terrible situations, they will lose perspective, lose confidence, and eventually lose hope if they feel isolated and alone. Don't let it happen. The earlier in the process you provide emotional support, the better, even if that simply means telling them to ask for help if they need it—and they will.

---

[4] For an excellent overview of 'self-serving bias' in a business context, see Bazerman, Loewenstein, and Moore, *Why Good Accountants do Bad Audits,* Harvard Business Review, November 2002.

Chapter 3

"We have met the enemy, and they are us."

A settlement negotiation is a long, oftentimes frustrating, and always stressful ordeal for borrowers. Different types of people (and creditors) approach the same situation in completely different ways. However, within the various types of creditors, the process can be remarkably consistent regardless of the amount in controversy.

In the first years of the Financial Crisis and ensuing Great Recession, the vast majority of problem loan cases involved builders, construction companies, and developers. But the types of clients have evolved as the real estate mess has sorted itself out. More recently, the types of businesses in distress is a more diverse group of real estate and operating companies.

As the banking crisis intensified in 2008 and 2009, fewer and fewer lenders remained open for new business or loans. With those banks that were still in the business of lending, underwriting criteria had changed dramatically for the worse. Borrowers saw a reduction of appraised values, lower loan-to-value ratios, increased collateral coverage requirements, and more onerous amortization, to name a few.

Borrowers, who oftentimes had never been turned down for credit, missed no payments, with strong credit scores and the ability to pay were unable to obtain loans. If loans were available, the more stringent requirements meant the borrower could not borrow sufficient funds to refinance the prior loan in full.

Applying what we learned from being involved with many hundreds of millions of dollars' worth of distressed debt, someone can explain a situation, and we can tell them exactly what is going to happen if they do nothing, and exactly what they must do to obtain the most favorable settlement.

If you could kick the person in the pants responsible for most of your trouble, you wouldn't sit for a month.

–Theodore Roosevelt

They won't listen, or they receive bad advice from their attorney, their accountant, or their friends at the country club. Borrowers tend to make the same mistakes in these situations, regardless of the company size, industry, or type of lender with whom they are dealing. Over and over, borrowers suffer harm from the same easily avoidable self-inflicted wounds:

(1) **Denial.** Borrowers finding us too late is not unusual. They have ignored the problem, hoped it would go away, complied with the creditors' demands to avoid confrontation, or hoped for a miracle. Borrowers use what liquidity that remains in their business for short-term extensions, fees, and principal reductions.

Unable to borrow what they owe, they tend to comply with the lender's demands until their liquidity is exhausted, and foreclosure, litigation, or bankruptcy are the only exit strategies left. However, we believe that there is no set of facts that can't be resolved; financial reality dictates the strategy, and experience drives the process.

(2) **Not Seeking Professional Help.** Workout and restructuring negotiation is a highly complicated process that is as much art as science. As much

psychology as math. The negotiation battle is fought on an ever-changing landscape—today's rejected proposal may be accepted 9 months later. This happens more than you know; we see it all the time. With experience, you eventually understand the regulatory constraints, the unspoken, but real, motivations and how the pressure points can change over time.

Negotiating a workout is entirely different from negotiating a loan or other financing. Few borrowers have ever been in a defaulted loan situation before and, unfortunately, will almost always make the wrong decision when trying to "work with the lender." Negotiating a settlement that is not only beneficial to the lender, but also feasible for the borrower, will require an experienced professional.

We worked on cases for borrowers dealing with FDIC receiverships, loss share banks, which have acquired failed banks in partnership with the FDIC, operating banks of all sizes, including money center, regional, and community banks, Commercial Mortgage-Backed Securities (CMBS) special servicers, insurance companies, individual loan purchasers and hedge funds that have purchased pools of loans from the FDIC or operating banks. Their game plan is always the same. We can predict exactly what will happen next and in what order, and when.

(3) *Not Understanding the Lender's Position and Goals.* Different types of lenders have different goals. Some are no more than debt collectors. Others have financial and/or regulatory constraints that guide their actions. Some are return-driven. By far the biggest misunderstanding borrowers have is how the lender seeks to minimize loss or maximize return.

Understanding the lender is a key component of the strategy based upon likely outcomes. You must learn and understand what the lender can or cannot do. Your lender's negotiation posture will be inflexible until you make your case and are persistent. The best thing to do is provide all of the information required, presented clearly and concisely, to promote acceptance of your proposal.

What changes in every case are the facts leading to the financial problems, and the personalities of the people involved. The former dictates the initial strategy, and the latter dictates the negotiating posture we will take. However, understanding the personalities of the other side takes time and effort, as well as patience.

To negotiate with someone, you must get to know them first. The asset manager doesn't bother with all of that because they already know what the borrower is: a liar and a cheater who could pay the loan but chooses not to because he thinks he can get away with it. Our job is to decide the best way to change the asset manager's mind.

(4) *Fear of Adversarial Situations:* Some creditors are more adversarial than others, pressuring the borrowers through tactics that may seem unfair. If negotiations become contentious, the borrower needs to be prepared to deal with the emotions. An emotionally charged confrontation between the borrower and lender is always a serious setback in the resolution process. An advisor with experience in the situations can help borrowers deal with the emotional and stressful nature of financial distress, remain objective, and negotiate with the lender without becoming contentious.

(5) *Too Much Advice:* The opposite of a borrower in denial or going it alone against the lender is seeking advice from too many sources, which can lead to paralysis. Friends and family, or business associates who "worked out their own loans," attorneys, accountants, former bankers, or other advisors will make the same mistakes most borrowers make. Reading articles and books on the subject, written by those same people, can cause the borrower to continue this cycle of error.

Many clients we represented were initially reluctant to hire our firm because they had previously hired a "workout consultant" who did not perform. Unless an advisor has specific experience with workouts and restructuring negotiation, we see entirely wrong assumptions about what action will cause which outcome.

For example, an attorney experienced in workouts and restructuring will understand that litigation is only one of many parts of the process. The key issue in the entire process is not victory/defeat in litigation, but collectability of judgment and/or recovery in bankruptcy. The entire process boils down to educating the lender on their recovery under various avenues.

The worst possible outcome is when the borrower's lawyer convinces them to quit midway through a negotiation process. In the most painful example, we had put the company in bankruptcy and were offering 70 cents on the dollar to settle, but the bank wanted 80 cents on the dollar. We could see the deal coming together—we needed the investor to make a higher offer, which was possible because the project's leasing team was doing a great job filling vacancies at higher rates.

What we needed was time, and we would get time if one of the partners would have the entity that held their partnership interest file for bankruptcy. Their bankruptcy attorney, despite our vehement objections and pleas to the contrary, convinced the partners to give up. He argued that spending more time and legal fees wasn't worth it because the bank was likely to prevail in the bankruptcy case.

Because they gave up, the partners lost millions in equity, the investor we sourced lost what would've been a great deal, and the bank certainly suffered a worse loss than they otherwise would have. A few people lost their jobs, and we lost the several hundred hours we spent working on this case. To add insult to injury, in a follow-up conversation with the bank's attorney we learned that the bank fully expected a bankruptcy and was shocked when it didn't happen.

(6) *Impatience.* Our clients are entrepreneurs who want to get deals done. With a large, bureaucratic institution, everything takes longer, and every decision is made via committee. Also, an "asset manager" for a bank or other lender is in a different situation from an average bank loan officer—they are overworked, underpaid, have little if any actual authority to settle cases, and can be frustrating to deal with because yours is one of dozens of cases to whom they are assigned.

You must understand the mindset of the asset manager and the lengthy process involved in debt restructuring. Patience is immensely important for a borrower. The lender's decision-making process is slow, and there is no way to speed up the process, apart from accepting an unfavorable outcome.

The ONLY times we had people lose projects or businesses or file for personal bankruptcy were the times where the client gave up, or if a prospective client didn't try. It happens. It happened more than once.

When a loan goes into default or for other reasons is classified as a special default risk, the people who work for the creditor with whom the borrower has a relationship go away. The loan file is transferred to the "special assets" department, and the lender's "workout" guys handle the loan thereafter. Unless somebody knows them from a former workout, nobody knows anybody. Everyone has their incorrect presumptions, but we do get a second chance at making a first impression. This requires significant analysis—what attitude would get us moving in the right direction? It's not a question you ever want to answer incorrectly.

Whose "honor," and honor to whom?

In today's world, honorable people allow themselves to suffer financial ruin because they honestly believe it's the honorable thing to do. And they have no choice but to be honorable, right? In the wake of the financial crisis, many people, almost 10,000 by some estimations,[5] took this principal to its (il)logical conclusion via suicide. The result is privation visited upon their families for the sake of avoiding conflict or, even worse, for the sake of keeping up appearances.

> *"Victory is always possible for the person who refuses to stop fighting."*
> –Napoleon Hill

Facing and confronting these challenges is too difficult for almost anyone. Borrowers want to take the path of least resistance and will agree to payment plans or settlements they cannot perform, ensuring financial ruin.

People commonly react with deep denial when financial trouble arrives, and in most cases they don't hire a lawyer. They keep busy scouring every hill and valley for precious cash to hand over to the bill collectors. Only after they run out of cash do most debtors realize that they need legal help. By then it's too late.

Meanwhile, the creditors/plaintiffs will assume the debtor has cash *somewhere* to pay the debt in full until proven otherwise. Creditors of all types will not hesitate to threaten their reputation and question their honor

---

[5] A. Reeves, M. McKee, D. Stuckler, *Economic suicides in the Great Recession in Europe and North America*, The British Journal of Psychiatry, June 2014

and character. The debtor, in a position of legal and emotional weakness, will accede to unreasonable demands.

The creditors' most effective weapons against debtors are not lawsuits, liens, or judgments. No, their most effective weapons are between the debtor's ears: emotions, particularly fear, intimidation, guilt, embarrassment, and shame.

Fear and intimidation: "We are bigger than you and have more resources to commit to collecting this debt."

Guilt: "Aren't you an honorable person who lives up to your agreements?"

Shame: "Don't you think you should do the right thing?"

Embarrassment: "We don't want this to get nasty and end up in court. Then it'll be public knowledge."

Creditors do this for one reason: it almost always works.

Chapter 4

"Don't you want to do the right thing?"

The lender and borrower go through a fairly consistent process, and our strategy and the ultimate outcome depends on facts, economics, the borrower's unique circumstances, the lender's unique circumstances, and unexpected events.

Creditors are structured and follow a set playbook. The *process* is what it's all about. Any large bureaucracy lives on process. Bureaucracies grind on slowly and are in a constant state of both internal and external conflict and disagreement.

Entrepreneurs are about substance. Entrepreneurs always have a sense of urgency but are surprisingly conflict averse. A sense of urgency ("I just want this to go away") and conflict aversion (exacerbated by not wanting to pay professional fees) will cost a borrower more money and pain in the long run.

The smarter option is working through the process and realizing that time is an ally. At the same time, they must not hesitate to forcefully assert legal rights wherever possible. "Fighting" means (1) making the other side prove its case in court, or (2) making the other side play by the rules.

Attorneys amaze us with their reluctance to do either. Corporate lawyers and business litigators will typically evaluate the legal case and negotiate a settlement based on their opinion as to whether you will win or lose in court. And if you win, will it be more or less than the anticipated legal fees? You signed a contract. You didn't perform. You will lose. You will pay. The outcome is considered a *fait accompli* – leaving no option but to accept. In reality, that is rarely the case in business disputes.

Most attorneys take a two-dimensional approach to their analysis, giving little thought to the more important dimensions, depth, and time. Business disputes are a poker game. You must follow the rules, but you must also play the odds, evaluate risks, and exploit mistakes; understanding your opponent in context is far more critical.

> *Sports are played mainly on a five-and-a-half-inch*
> *court, the space between your ears.*
>
> –Bobby Jones

The Creditor's Secret Weapon

Lawyers who are not prepared and willing to fight the battle against their client's emotions have no business representing them. In debtor/creditor situations, and most other civil litigation, frankly, the legal merits of the case are largely irrelevant. Meanwhile, most lawyers are always in the mode of "cover-your-own-ass."

So the lawyer sketches out to the client the worst case scenario: huge legal bills, losing the case, judgments, collections, losing the house, filing for bankruptcy, the lender taking and auctioning family heirlooms. This feeds a debtor's fears. The attorney is doing the creditor's job for them.

The borrower just wants all of this to go away and, thanks to their legal counsel, avoiding the worst-case scenario is all that matters. They will agree to impossible terms, and the creditor doesn't care.

The lender isn't concerned about whether the borrower can perform. The asset manager closes the file and will work on other matters until the borrower defaults on the settlement. If the creditor was smart, they secured the settlement with a consent judgment for the full amount. When the borrower runs out of cash, and can't perform the settlement, the borrower is finished. If the creditor doesn't have a consent judgment, they'll run the same game again, and legal counsel will give the same "cover-your-own-ass" advice to the client, resulting in the same conclusion.

However, legal counsel is duty bound to explain all of the possible outcomes, including the worst-case scenario, and goodness knows no lawyer wants to discuss the likelihood of different outcomes for fear of malpractice liability. But by maintaining the professional and ethical standards, the attorney makes their client, already an emotional basket case, even more terrified. This does the creditor's work for them. What do you do?

Don't fear, prepare. Do not hide the truth. These are the two most important pieces of advice we give a client in financial trouble.

Do Not Fear. Prepare.

Find out what you're afraid of, and go live there.

–Chuck Palahniuk, author of *Fight Club*

Being prepared to lose everything is one of the most effective means of preventing bankruptcy. The true value to the borrower in being prepared to file for bankruptcy is how this mental preparation takes away the power of the threat.

The creditors are hoping the borrower stays in denial; denial means they'll eventually get all the cash and the collateral, too. However, most collections people don't think about it this way. They use the debtor's emotions against them (fear, guilt, shame, embarrassment, etc.) whether they realize it or not.

This preparation has two distinct parts. The first is understanding the psychological warfare that the creditor will employ, and embracing the ensuing emotions as perfectly normal. By facing the threat and preparing for it, you'll be able to make the emotional power of the threat, and the fear it induces, go away.

Borrowers should go through the mental process of what exactly they would do if they had to file for bankruptcy liquidation. What if they lost their house, cars, jewelry, etc., and had to start all over again? Embrace this possibility and prepare for it emotionally.

> *"Now wait a minute. We lawyers are berated and blamed for defeat because we explain the worst-case scenario, and the advice I get is to have my client assume they'll go bankrupt?"*

We aren't talking about the same thing. By having the client make decisions based upon *avoiding* the worst-case scenario, the attorney is feeding the fear. Having the client *embrace* the possibility, to *not fear* the worst-case scenario, and to *prepare* for it, takes away the fear's power.

> *I've had a lot of worries in my life,*
> *most of which never happened.*
>
> – Mark Twain

They don't teach this kind of bedside manner in law school—lawyers must educate, demonstrate, or remind the client that even if they did have to file for bankruptcy, everything will be okay. They *will* make it, the crisis will be resolved, they will move on, recover, and all of this will be a distant memory. They will get a clean start, time marches on, and they can't take away family and friends.

This kind of advice may save someone's life.

The second part of the preparation, the other essential half of the equation, is actually preparing for bankruptcy. Don't put it off, stay in denial, and hope for the best.

If your legal counsel cannot clearly explain the bankruptcy process, in layman's terms, find an attorney who can. People do not understand the bankruptcy process, even if they're sophisticated businessmen, or even if they've been in a bankruptcy case previously. In speaking with hundreds of clients and prospective clients over the years, not one understood what bankruptcy means, what their rights are, the procedures, etc. The vast majority of clients do not even know the difference between Chapter 7 and Chapter 11. Moreover, people don't understand that filing for bankruptcy doesn't render them helpless. In reality, filing for bankruptcy protection seizes control of the situation from the creditors.

Do Not Hide the Truth

In the period 2008-2012, the real estate business was awful. There were two types of real estate owners and developers after the Financial Crisis: the people who were wiped out or at least took a big, unimaginable hit to their net worth. The other group was the people who were too proud to admit they did, too.

"Everything's GREAT. BEST YEAR EVER!"

Especially in the world of commercial collections against business owners, embarrassment and shame are the sharpest knives in the creditor's drawer. The debtors may not fear losing everything because they are in denial. They may not fear bankruptcy because they are resolved to never file for bankruptcy no matter what.

What keeps them awake at night? What others will say (WOWS).

You see, the financially distressed borrower has been telling everyone, perhaps even his spouse, that his world is one of rainbows and unicorns. His Facebook page is splashed with happy pictures of summer vacation hiking in Wyoming, or the kids fishing off the pier in Nantucket Harbor. Sailing in the Caribbean. Mom and dad with friends at the black tie fundraiser for the museum.

Related to WOWS is DTRT—Doing the right thing.

- Doing the *right* thing to construct the life that *everyone* says you should strive to reach.

- Living the *right* way by accumulating useless junk, living in the *right* neighborhood, sending the kids to the *right* school and belonging to the *right* country club.

- Striving to achieve the *right* goals set for you not because you aspire to them but because that's what everyone else says you should do.

- Measuring your self-worth by your net worth relative to others.

Where do you eventually go when you achieve all these goals and obtain all of these things? You go in a casket. Or an urn. Doubtless in the "right" cemetery...

Combine the terror of what others will say with the enormous pressure creditors apply to do the right thing, and the pressure on the borrower to pay debts they should not pay can become unbearable. Middle and upper middle class men are particularly susceptible to these tactics.

Effective collectors know this. You know this.

For example, why do process servers serve lawsuits on Saturday morning? Mostly for maximum psychological impact.

Appear at points which the enemy must hasten to defend; march swiftly to places where you are not expected." – Sun Tzu, The Art of War

On Saturday mornings, the husband is usually gone doing errands or spending time on the golf course or tennis court. The wife is getting the kids together to go swimming or to the mall, and there's the process server, waiting in the driveway.

A person in this situation should be honest with people about the shape they're in. Stop lying about rainbows and unicorns. They should not be ashamed to admit to close friends and family members that they are in great danger. When people are honest about being in difficult times, they find support and encouragement, not shame. They get the most help from people and places they least expect; people will surprise you with their generosity.

Also, as you might also know from personal experience, when you admit your failings, you discover who your true friends are. As a bonus, and at no extra charge, you rid yourself of those who were friends because of what you have, not the person you are.

Unintended Consequences of Keeping Up Appearances

Pretending everything is great to others also hurts the communication strategy with the creditors. You should be painting an accurate financial picture and showing why your proposal is generous, will likely yield the creditors more than litigation and collections net of expenses, and is also a plan that the borrower can accomplish.

What will your creditors think when we are showing them that you, Mr. Client, have little to no cash, but in public you act as if you are better than ever?

When the borrower is running around spending money keeping up appearances, you should assume that word will get back to the lender. It may not, but you never know. The fellow at the cocktail party listening in on you recounting last week's deep sea fishing trip to Mexico could be your banker's next door neighbor. Do you still order the surf and turf on your weekly trip to the town's best steakhouse? Is Mrs. Client showing off her new jewelry to her tennis group at the club?

The collections people are digging. If the borrower's actions outside the meeting rooms are inconsistent with financial reality, they will assume the borrower is lying to them. They have to. You would, too. When the borrower arrives at the meeting to plead poverty in a 7-series BMW, they will notice. It won't matter that the car is 10 years old and breaks down twice a week because the owner can't afford necessary maintenance.

Being truthful about your situation with friends and cutting expenses and living within limited means has no downside except injured pride. Convincing the borrower to drop the façade is tough. Very tough. They won't always listen. But when you succeed, you take away the other side's most effective, least expensive, weapons.

. . . . .

"So Gary's construction company made good profits, enough to support a comfortable upper middle class lifestyle, but it wasn't enough, was it?"

The credit card debt piled up. We were like everyone else—trying to live a lifestyle a bit out of reach for us financially. We didn't prepare for an economic downturn, and when construction work disappeared, we didn't immediately change our spending habits. Gary never did, even after we ran out of money.

The Media and Entertainment Industry reinforces the notion that being content with one's economic status is akin to admitting failure and having given up trying. Many people, regardless of wealth, aspire to accumulate more wealth, but few do anything about it, and even fewer succeed.

There I was in 2012, separated from my husband, with two kids, no money, three jobs and a mountain of debt, moving back into my Mom's house. I was in my mid-thirties, and when I was younger, I thought I would be living 'happily ever after' by that age.

Instead I was broke and living with my Mom. I thought my world couldn't get worse. Then Gary killed himself.

This idea of perpetual seeking of higher socioeconomic status isn't as pervasive in other countries. On the other hand, American entrepreneurial culture created the largest economy, and by far the most prosperous society in history. Few people understand that even in the Colonial Period, on the eve of the American Revolution, the standard of living in the American Colonies was at or above any other country in the world.[6] America has always been that way.

However, the more stuff you accumulate, the more you have to lose, particularly when you bought your accumulated stuff with borrowed money.

---

[6] Jack P. Greene, *Pursuits of Happiness: The Social Development of Early Modern British Colonies and the Formation of American Culture* (University of North Carolina Press, 1998), p. 182.

Part 2

"No enemy is worse than bad advice."

–Sophocles

Chapter 5

"I am confident I will collect every penny."

February, 2012

Two gentlemen bought a large piece of raw land in rural Arkansas and made all of their payments out-of-pocket because there was no cash flow. Their bank failed, and a new bank acquired their loan in a loss-share transaction with the FDIC. When the loan matured, the asset manager demanded a 10 percent principal reduction for a 90-day renewal. When they asked the asset manager what would happen in 90 days, they were told that the bank would consider renewing it, with another principal reduction. The businessmen did the math and called us.

Our clients' primary business was construction on large commercial projects. They had many contingent liabilities, loans they had guaranteed, and their income was a fraction of what it was before the financial crisis. The value of the land had declined precipitously, and the loan was deeply underwater. Whether it was a 90-day renewal or a nine-month renewal, making large principal reductions every few months would drain all of their cash. When there was no more cash to pay for renewals, the bank would foreclose anyway and sue them for the deficiency.

One of the partners epitomized the image of the genteel Southern Gentleman. His business had been in the family for generations. This partner had real estate income but had cut rents to not only keep his properties occupied, but also to help keep his tenants in business. The family business was his only asset, and the company was losing money, had little work, and was unlikely to survive.

Commercial construction lags the real economy for months if not years because of the time involved in putting product (buildings) on the market. However, when the economy recovers, commercial construction is one of the last sectors to come back because first the excess capacity from the prior expansion must be absorbed, then the construction lag time. The situation was different in the Great Recession. Construction projects stopped. In normal circumstances, a lender would continue to fund construction draws to get the project completed and thereby protect its collateral. A half-completed building is worth less than the amount invested at that point because of the high cost of resuming construction, degradation of the structure, and changes in design.

However, when the project's lender is a bank that fails, construction is over. As banks failed *en masse* in the Great Recession, this became a huge problem. The FDIC wasn't going to fund construction draws, and the government sold many of the loans to investment funds who could fund construction draws, but the loan sales agreements and documents didn't obligate them (and the borrower was in default anyway). The "loss-share bank" system exacerbated the problem. Those banks were not only under no obligation to fund any construction, they were specifically obligated to liquidate the loan and, if necessary, the collateral.

The other partner was a caricature of The Millionaire Next Door—self-made, nerves of steel, success was always his destiny, but still just an ol' country boy driving an old pickup truck (except for the $10 million in a trust fund, the 200-acre hunting plantation, and vague references to an antique car collection, whereabouts unknown). Like Robert Duvall's character Colonel Kilgore in *Apocalypse Now,* "he just knew he would get out of this without so much as a scratch." Over the years, he had done significant estate planning and had significant assets. However, the assets were held in a family limited partnership in which he is a minority interest holder. Trusts hold other real estate assets. This borrower doesn't have any assets that the bank can reach—none of those entities are borrowers or guarantors.

Over the years he had made significant transfers of assets into his wife's name, but we could substantiate the value given, and she also had ownership interests in his businesses from the beginning. She wasn't a borrower. Absent a long and costly fraudulent transfer lawsuit, the lender could not reach her assets. The original bank never required any of the trusts, limited partnerships, etc., to guarantee the loans, and if they had, the governing documents of the trusts or partnerships prohibited such guarantees.

Why did the bank make a loan to a man with no assets in his name? The first reason is his construction business was generating fantastic income when the lender made the loan—the company worked on major infrastructure projects and large office buildings, shopping malls, and the like.

The second reason the original bank made this loan was willful blindness. The loan officer wants to make the loan and move on to the next deal (after collecting the fees of which the loan officer gets a piece). The dynamics of a loan origination are different than most imagine. The loan officer is adverse to his loan committee in many respects; he needs justifications from the borrower to overcome the objections of superiors, which the borrowers cheerfully explain away, not realizing that they may be sowing the seeds for their own demise by getting loans for which they aren't qualified.

The guys locating the borrowers to whom the bank lends money don't want to know about any problems. That's not to say they don't care at all—of course they could lose their job making too many loans that go bad, but this wasn't a concern in the mid-2000s as we all know. Nobody had such concerns when the bank made this loan. The borrower's company had seven-or-eight-figure annual net income every year for a decade or more.

In this case, the borrowers had personal relationships with the bank president (this was a small, rural community bank), so the underwriting' is based on the borrower's good name. He is good for it. This was a $3 million loan on a piece of raw land that the borrowers plan to use for recreational purposes—the collateral will *never* generate any income.

The originating bank didn't take the time to understand how this borrower structured his assets. In many instances, borrowers will put assets on a loan application owned by their wives, trusts, or limited liability companies. The banks did not dig into these numbers, particularly the community banks that ended up failing, as was the case here.

And not just the failed bank. The acquiring bank did not dig into the various limited liability companies to see what they owned.

This loss-share bank, with whom we tangled many times, obviously did not even do an Internet search of our client. If they had, they would've discovered that one of the LLCs owned by one of the trusts held a controlling interest in a professional sports team. Not an NFL or NBA team, mind you, but still. The team had a website; he was shown as the owner of the franchise. Photographs of him smiling with the team after a big win. We kept waiting for the phone to ring with the "WHAT THE FRESH HELL IS THIS?" call from the asset manager. The phone never rang.

The team wasn't very successful, which would've made the situation with the lender even worse because the owner, our client, was still funding cash shortfalls for the team while we are negotiating a discount with this particular lender. Now, as always we were prepared for its eventual discovery. The borrower's "ownership" of the team was so remote that no creditor could ever reach it through him. He was only the *de facto* owner. Legally, he owned nothing and was only the CEO of the franchise. However, more than one phone call did need to be made to tell him to stay away from TV cameras at events, not to do any interviews, take down websites, etc.

The asset manager would've had a fit. The special assets officers and their committees get angry that a wealthy person is "getting away" with not paying their debts. *Well, it's your own fault, Charlie Brown.* The original lender's underwriting was sloppy and you bought the loan. It's your baby.

They were angry enough already without knowing about the sports franchise. The successor bank was local, not out of state. They knew our borrowers, and our borrowers ran hard and lived big when times were good. The asset manager was going to tighten the vise on these boys until somebody coughed up the money, but they had no idea who they were dealing with. This particular client was our best client ever. He never called us unless he had a real issue. His "I don't give a shit about anything" attitude wasn't an act. He knew his assets were protected; the asset manager would never break him—the bank wouldn't come close. It took about two years for them to realize this.

After our clients stopped paying and wouldn't agree to any more extensions or principal reductions, the bank filed a lawsuit. The case wasn't unusual—we sent the lender everything they asked for, and they didn't look at any of it. The litigation progressed, but the asset manager did agree to mediation.

Settling a case at mediation is rare but still a productive exercise. We will get close to settling but don't quite get there. But that's all right. It's an opportunity for the two sides to get to know one another and interact. The presence of the mediator holds down tempers, which is nice.

The mediator, a retired trial court judge, asked the lawyers to give an opening statement. The bank's lawyer went first. He was a young, lumpy fellow with a crew cut and an ill-fitting brown suit. Lawyers tend to share the temperament of their clients and vice versa. This case was a prime example.

The bank lawyer's opening statement was a spirited advocacy of the bank's legal and moral right to prevail in the case, and, the lawyer added, "In this case, particularly, I am confident that after we obtain the judgment I will collect every penny the defendants owe my client."

Our client's lawyer burst out laughing. She was younger than the other participants in the mediation, and the derisive laughter caught everyone by surprise, and we thought, "Oh boy, here we go."

The mediator saved the day. "Well counselor, I've practiced law and been a judge for over 30 years, and if you collect 100 percent of a judgment, you'll be the first lawyer who ever does it and probably the last."

Although the mediator bluntly put the bank's lawyer in his place, the episode meant that this mediation was going nowhere. The bank's lawyer was mad now.

The big problem with the case was that the special assets officers with whom we worked (three or four different ones; this bank's turnover was incredible) could not understand the structure of the client's personal financial statement. He had several million dollars in cash in an account, and the asset managers expected him to write them a check. But he couldn't do that. The funds were the proceeds from the sale of a company, and the parties structured the sale transaction (to make a long story short) a certain way for tax purposes, and if he liquidated the account before a certain time, the taxes and penalties would leave him with nothing after paying the bank.

The asset managers couldn't understand the complicated tax structure, but eventually they understood that the borrower would die on this hill. After almost a year, the bank won a motion for summary judgment against the guarantors. We cooperated with all the post judgment discovery, interrogatories, and depositions. We explained numerous times that one partner had lost everything, and the other's assets were long ago placed in family trusts or pledged as collateral for other loans. This meant that for different reasons, collecting anything from our clients would be difficult if not impossible.

Meanwhile, we thought we knew what the bank would ultimately take to settle the deal. In one of the calls with the bank's first asset manager (three or four asset managers previously), he gave us the bank's appraisal number as a justification for the amount of the principal payment the bank demanded. Our clients were not willing to cough up the appraised value in cash to keep the property, and the bank clearly had no intention of foreclosing on the property—they had enough foreclosed land already. They were coming after the guarantors.

A judgment doesn't mean you will lose everything you have. A judgment is not a guarantee of payment, only a license for the creditor to attempt to collect, and if you don't have large sums of cash or unencumbered liquid assets, a judgment isn't going to change that. Lenders and tax collectors know this as well as anyone else.

However, if you do have a large amount of cash, the lender will be able to take it, but they must get the judgment first (unless it's in a bank account at their bank and the loan provides a right of setoff, which almost certainly it does). Either way, if the borrower has cash, they had best be prepared to give all or most of that cash to the creditors. They may not have to, but they should prepare for it.

That being said, if the client had a large amount of unprotected cash or other liquid assets, we would have used an entirely different strategy from the very beginning.

Our clients wanted to keep that land, but getting a discount and keeping the property is difficult and tricky and must be precisely structured, and the bank had too many hard feelings. They weren't going to let the rich guys keep this land. The clients did locate a buyer for the property, but the offer was several hundred thousand dollars less than the bank's appraisal. We convinced the client to come up with the cash to bridge the gap. They would be out of the $3 million debt at around 40 cents on the dollar. Meanwhile, someone at the bank who understood the tax structures and other protected assets managed to stumble into the deal, and the bank agreed to the settlement.

Both of the client's businesses survived and are thriving again thanks to the newest construction boom. This case appeared complex because understanding our client's financial structure was difficult, but the whole time the case was as simple as they come. Our clients were tough, seasoned in the rough-and-tumble world of the construction industry. They didn't scare easily. We had less work managing their emotions and more work managing the lender's emotions.

The successful resolution came back to the two core missions in the workout: convince the lender that you are telling the truth, and show the lender that you will never give up. Ever. The latter wasn't an issue, and the former needed time and for the right person at the bank to look at the structures and understand they were bulletproof.

Chapter 6

"A Settlement Mutually Unsatisfactory to All Parties"

April, 2009

Not many months before it failed, Alpha Bank and Trust, located in suburban Atlanta, was the fastest-growing start-up bank in the country. Because of its rapid growth, Alpha Bank was unable to weather the storm that struck the industry. When it failed, the client received a letter from the FDIC. He was informed that he had six months to refinance his loan with another lender, or the FDIC would sell the loan on the open market.

As a financial boom turns to bust, most commercial borrowers are in a position where if their bank fails, they can liquidate stocks and bonds, or CDs, or even bank accounts to pay off the loans. But by the time banks start failing, the stock market has crashed and the credit markets halted. Everyone has liquidity problems, not enough cash, and other real estate investments that have lost value in addition to being illiquid.

The borrower will be highly frustrated. They may have never been turned down for a loan before but now cannot get one. They may have never missed a payment on a loan but are frightened they will have to file for bankruptcy.

Not long before the bank failed, our client could have liquidated his stock portfolio and paid this loan off. However, with the market crash, this was no longer an option.

He was scared and did not know what to do. He did not want his credit ruined with a foreclosure. The small office building he built was 75 to 80 percent leased and generated enough cash flow to pay the operating expenses and debt service. Alpha Bank and Trust had agreed to give him a 36-month loan to bridge the gap until he refinanced his construction note. However, Alpha Bank failed before that loan was finalized, and the FDIC was under no obligation to renew it.

The FDIC's position was, "We want to get paid our $2 million, or we are going to sell the note." Nobody realized that the banking system was collapsing. Other banks were rolling up the mat and were not lending any money. The client's primary business was a family-operated company. With orders down and in need of cash infusions, it was unclear how long he could feed that business until it became cash flow positive again.

The client was also extremely frustrated; he had never missed a payment or been turned down for a loan in his life. He was scared that this was going to drive him into bankruptcy, or worse drive him out of business—that everything he owned and had worked so hard for was crumbling.

Eventually the parties scheduled a meeting to discuss options. When the lender wants to meet with you, what you must do is not only make your case, but also do their job for them to achieve a favorable settlement.

After gathering the necessary information, we create a detailed personal financial statement and compare it to the person's financial situation when the lender originally underwrote the loan. We need to be prepared to explain all of the changes to the client's financial situation, in detail, with backup documentation. Why are the differences there?

We always hear the question of whether to provide all of the requested financial information, and the answer is almost always yes. You want the asset manager to work with you in making decisions. You must give them information to do so. You may believe that portions of the financial disclosure will hurt the borrower's position. If so, you will need to provide a detailed explanation as to why the lender should not hold that information against the borrower.

Make sure you understand any transactions that the lender will find suspicious: for example, large cash withdrawals, small but repeated cash withdrawals over a long period, and particularly assets that appear on the original statements used in underwriting the loan that are not on the current financial statements you submit. The asset manager looks for those items first.

Be prepared to deliver tax returns and backup account statements to support every line in the company financial information as well as the personal financial statement. Depending on the situation, historical financials or even financial projections for the next two to three years may be appropriate.

The main goal is to bury the lender in information. When you bury the other side in information, all of which you thoroughly understand and they are seeing for the first time, you have the advantage. When executed properly, you become the lender's source for explanation of why things are.

Keep documentation organized, and provide the information to the lender in the most idiot-proof format possible. Despite your best efforts, be prepared to send and re-send the same information over and over again. Bureaucracies live on paperwork and paper shuffling, but the disorganization can be staggering, not to mention discouraging.

In one case we had been trying to help a client keep a project going, keep investors or potential new lenders interested in the deal, preparing cash flow projections, etc., and received a call from the asset manager asking for the third time about title documentation for an airplane the guarantor sold three years ago. We had to stop working on important matters to dig out the old email with the documentation and a written explanation of that transaction and how the borrower received no proceeds because he only owned 1/6th of the plane and the cost of repairs exceeded the amount *of equity the partners had in the old crate anyway. Bankers in particular have a fixation on airplanes. Airplanes and boats make them angry.[7] We were trying to save a company with over 100 employees, and the banker wants to re-discuss the airplane and the boat.*

In our case, the guarantor's operating company had declining revenue and negative cash flow, and the owners were putting in additional capital to keep the business going. We provided a projection of the length of time required to get the company cash flow positive before debt service. We also underwrote a hypothetical financing, which considered the other usual bank underwriting ratios, such as debt service coverage or fixed charge coverage.

Putting in this additional capital by the guarantors, affects the lender even if the loan is in default for nonpayment. Although staying in business may help the lender in the long run if things work out, at the same time the guarantor's ability to pay a settlement, or for the creditor to collect on a judgment, declines. The best point to make in this situation is emphasizing that the company cannot stand on its own, so it has no value to any purchaser or investor except for the discounted value of its hard assets and possibly an abstract value of its intellectual property rights. In other words, basically no value. This may keep the negotiations going.

As the negotiation with the FDIC plodded along, we sourced a hard-money lender, which was willing to lend $900,000 on the asset, although the loan would take second positions on the guarantor's personal residences.

This was the only potential source of financing at the time. No bank was lending on real estate, and unstabilized exurban office buildings were only slightly above residential pipe farms to potential lenders.

---

[7] *Airplanes and boats make creditors angry, particularly bankers, because they see the borrower who is not paying them but is retaining his badges of wealth. They assume the borrower is expending large amounts of cash for use, repairs, and upkeep, instead of selling them and giving the cash to the creditors. Selling the asset at that time may or may not be a good idea because of price volatility. The price of aircraft in particular will crater in a bad economy because they are expensive to own, but when the economy recovers, general aviation aircraft see high demand and high prices. The same applies to boats. However, in our experience the borrower's attitude about the boat is usually "PLEASE come take away that floating money pit."*

The terms were typical of a hard-money loan: fifty percent loan-to-value. 12-month term, borrower pays a 5 percent origination (loan) fee, 15 percent interest, and all closing costs. The good news was the interest, fees, and costs would be rolled into the loan, and there would be no payments until a balloon payment at maturity. This would solve the short-term cash flow issues. The bad news was that the balloon payment would be over $1.1 million for this $900,000 financing. A nearly 23 percent cost of capital. But the hard-money lender was the only game in town, and we had a solid game plan for a takeout loan at maturity.

After over six months of meetings with the FDIC, they concluded that the best alternative was the hard-money lender lending the client $900,000 in satisfaction of the $2 million note.

"They concluded..." Did you notice that?

Nonetheless, the client was ecstatic. He was relieved not to get sued. When initially confronted by the FDIC and this predicament, he was scared to death. In the end, he was thrilled to have a chance to hang onto property and keep all of his businesses moving forward.

We don't expect a high five, home run for our borrower to thumb their nose at the lender. Usually, the settlement results in the lender getting more than they could have gotten if they pursued and obtained a judgment against the client and forced the client into bankruptcy. But the borrower can't escape without feeling pain, too, especially if they have any liquid assets remaining of any value. Sometimes we were lucky, but the settlement is often what we call "mutually unsatisfactory."

Chapter 7

"We aren't allowed to talk to you unless you bring the loan current."

Lenders will not refinance a loan for many possible reasons, even if doing so is in their best interest, and different lenders/note holders will approach the same situation differently. Understanding these distinctions and motivations is critical.

Almost any lender will offer only short-term renewals at higher interest rates coupled with demands for principal payments, which hurt the borrower's liquidity position in these situations: (1) the collateral is worth less than the loan balance, (2) the guarantor's financial strength has declined since the lender made the original loan, (3) the original lender sold your loan, and you are negotiating with the loan purchaser, or (4) the original lender was a bank that failed.

Sometimes the reasons have nothing to do with the borrower or the loan. The lender may be reducing certain types of loans in its portfolio. This often happens with non-recourse lenders such as insurance companies and investment banks. This situation can lead to outstanding outcomes for the borrower.

The strategy you employ will depend in no small part on the goals of your creditors. Some are no more than debt collectors. Others, banks in particular, have financial and/or regulatory constraints that guide their actions. Investment funds and debt buyers are return-driven.

By far the biggest misunderstanding clients have is how creditors seek to minimize loss or maximize return. Understanding the adversary is a key component of any strategy. What affects the adversary that is not contained within the four corners of the contract? Are there external factors unrelated to your relationship or this dispute that may affect the adversary's goals? These questions always make a difference.

You will be at a distinct advantage when you understand regulatory pressures, what regulators and government bureaucracies want, how they want presentations to look, and the current acceptable parameters for restructuring or extending existing credit.

Financial institutions will use the "all-mighty regulators" as an "appeal to authority" argument in negotiations with borrowers. "We can't do _____ because regulations forbid it." This tactic almost always works. Think about it in your own financial life.

Financial institutions and other large companies will exaggerate the amount of power the regulators have over their decision making. Understanding the requirements can keep you from making critical errors. By and large, the regulators will not object to the *substance* of the resolution, so long as the resolution is "commercially reasonable."

This is a political term: for a regulator, "commercially reasonable" means "nothing in this deal will draw the ire of my boss, the media, or a politician." Assume any objections to the structure of a given proposal on account of regulations are posturing by the lender.

Procedurally, however, the regulator's stance is very different. Again, procedure over substance for bureaucracies, and substance over procedure for entrepreneurs. As an example, a financial institution must collect certain documents such as tax returns, 1099s/W-2 statements, K-1 forms, and so on. The lender must collect the same sorts of documentation that one would collect when making a loan in the first place. You won't get away with not providing tax returns; however, you probably will not have to provide balance sheets and income statements for every LLC the borrower may own or of which the borrower is a member (except when the entity is the borrower on the loan).

Bombing the Rubble

"It's hard to get a sense that you are advancing the [Vietnam] war effort when you are prevented from doing anything more than bouncing the rubble of an utterly insignificant target. ... In all candor, we thought our civilian commanders were complete idiots who didn't have the least notion of what it took to win the war." –John McCain, Faith of My Fathers, p. 185 (1999)

The next financial crisis, and we *will* have one, will catch the regulators unprepared, either from having a plan to address the coming problem, from a pure lack of resources to address the problem, or most likely both. The U.S. has had two waves of bank failures in the past 30 years, and we know what works and what does not work, more or less.

In the 1980s Savings and Loan crisis, the government formed the Resolution Trust Corporation to assume control over all of the assets of the failed Savings & Loans. The RTC "bad bank" strategy remains the least-bad option. In 2009, however, the government wanted to find a way to do better.

Online auctions had good results, but had huge overhead and transaction costs. Furthermore, privacy issues abounded. The auction company provided documentation with respect to loans to us that contained personal financial statements of guarantors who were friends or acquaintances.

The "loss-share bank" debacle deserves a book all its own. An acquiring bank would purchase all of the assets of a failed bank in partnership with the FDIC and was charged with liquidating all of the collateral (the agreements with the FDIC forbid sale of the loan itself absent a byzantine approval process) at a "commercially reasonable value" after "exhausting all collections remedies" within a given time frame, typically five to nine years. Loss share banks acquired over 300 failed institutions, and the results (in our experience) have been disastrous for the borrowers.

The FDIC also entered into so-called "structured sales" of loans with private equity firms such as Blackstone, Colony Capital, Lone Star Funding, and Rialto Capital. The results have been good for the FDIC and spectacular for the private equity (PE) firms (Blackstone, Lone Star and Colony are the first, second, and fourth largest PE firms as of 2014), who rake in hundreds of millions of dollars in asset management fees on top of their equity investment in partnership with the FDIC (in reality, zero-interest financing of the purchase).

And in some cases, particularly early in the aftermath of the Financial Crisis, the FDIC receiver itself would settle the loans directly with the borrowers. Surprisingly, FDIC receivers are the easiest to deal with and often approach the workout process reasonably and rationally. Part of the reason is political: the FDIC exists to protect the borrowers, not maximize their return on the purchased loan.

Also, the borrowers are constituents of the government and are therefore, at least nominally, the ultimate authority to whom the regulator reports. Yes, we understand this sounds farcical, but the FDIC doesn't want bad press, which they will get if they mistreat bank customers. On the other hand, the private equity firms and loss-share banks can screw over the borrowers with reckless abandon with little to no media coverage.[8]

The regulators fear the politicians and ultimately the voters, and the asset managers fear the regulators, nominally. The loss-share bank's number one goal is to not draw any attention of the regulators to any settlement transactions it completes. This is why loss-share banks were/are inflexible.

The private equity groups, however, enjoy the fruits of regulatory capture[9] and have less concern about the fate of the borrowers and otherwise no concern about anything other than hitting their return on investment goals. One would think that private equity asset managers would approach

---

[8] Believe us. We tried. We hired media consultants to push our clients' experiences with bank failures and loss-share banks in local TV news media. The consistent response from the media (and the consultants, for that matter) was the situation was too complex to explain in a 3-minute news story.

[9] "Regulatory Capture" is a form of political corruption that occurs when a regulatory agency, created to act in the public interest, instead advances the commercial or political concerns of special interest groups that dominate the industry or sector it is charged with regulating." –definition from *Wikipedia*

these cases in a more rational way, but most don't. Why? Hiring.

What? Hiring? Yes. When the large private equity firms acquire large distressed debt portfolios, they have to staff up with bodies to handle the workload. And these people are typically who? They are former bankers, that's who.

So the private equity asset manager likely a former banker with experience as an in-house special asset professional. Therefore, that person is going to approach collecting, restructuring, etc., in the same way the banks do it. Loss-share banks are the same.

This is why, by and large, the loan workout game plan doesn't change no matter the lender or owner of the loan. With commercial loans, the game plan is essentially the same regardless of the loan amount. What changes the strategy in each workout is the facts of the case and the personalities involved.

The best asset managers are former real estate folks or people from industries other than financial services because they can understand the borrower's difficulties and look at values and transaction costs with the proper perspective. They tend to be the toughest negotiators, but it's worth it.

Relying on Assurances by the Asset Manager? Don't.

Do not rely on anything the people working for the lenders say. Not promises, assurances, statements of fact, statements of opinion—nothing. Until the parties sign documents modifying the loan, or a closing occurs that releases all collateral, or the banking relationship otherwise terminates, the ONLY thing you can rely on are the lender covenants and requirements in the loan documents signed at the original closing.

The borrower may have a claim or action or defense against the bank if someone at the bank made a promise upon which the borrower relied to their detriment. Occasionally, you may have a claim to pursue, based heavily on facts and testimony. The claim's chances of prevailing on the merits of this claim are remote, but that's okay.

The fact that you have a legal defense or counterclaim is great leverage against lenders because they cannot afford to lose those types of claims.

Also, the claim inserts more uncertainty into the process, and more importantly it means more time and expense related to the collection for the lender.

October, 2011

The lender that loaned our client the purchase money for his building failed, and another bank took over the loan. When he emailed the acquiring bank to determine the contact for his loan, he received an email back saying they could not locate his file in their system and that he should not make any payments until they found it.

Six months after the loss-share bank told him to stop paying, they contacted him to notify him that they found his file, but they would not talk to him until he brought his loan current. Amazingly (and foolishly), he made six months' worth of payments, plus interest to bring the account to current status, and resumed making payments.

This ploy is extremely effective: "we can't talk unless you bring the loan current" or "you must first sign this pre-negotiation agreement waiving all claims and defenses against us, and we can discuss your loan."

Ninety days later, he told the bank he needed a renewal. The bank wanted to change his loan terms from a 30-year amortization to a 15-year amortization (a payment he couldn't afford), plus they wanted a 20 percent principal payment (money he did not have). If he refused, they would advertise his building for foreclosure. The bank officer did say that if he paid the bank a fee of $15,000 (that would not be applied to principal or interest, just a fee), they would postpone foreclosure that month. He paid it.

We became involved the next month, when the building was about to be foreclosed on again and he could not work out a renewal. He had a paper trail of all of his interactions with the employees of the bank. However, time was short, and the bank was not interested in negotiating further.

Prior to the foreclosure date, we filed a bankruptcy of the entity that owned the property, which canceled the foreclosure. Thanks to victories on a few key initial motions, our client retained control of the property, and he was able to operate it. Commensurate with the filing in bankruptcy court, the client filed a lawsuit against the bank in state court under various lender liability causes of action, which provided negotiation leverage.

The bankruptcy and lawsuit ground on for months, but the bank did return to the negotiating table, and we worked out a deal. In exchange for our client dismissing the lawsuit, they agreed to cut the interest rate to 5 percent with monthly payments of interest plus a $1,000/month principal payment. The income from the property could support this payment. Most importantly, the bank agreed to release the guarantors.

Our client's diligence in keeping all of his email correspondence with the bank was key to the outcome. Because this bank took actions that they should not have taken, among them the "fee" demanded and instructing him to default on the loan, we were able to put the pressure on the bank, which resulted in a positive outcome for our client.

Explore lender liability possibilities with legal counsel if the borrower can allege any of the following acts by the lender:

- *Appreciably altering its procedures for calculating credit availability or reporting requirements when the debtor fell into financial difficulty;*

- *Contravening its loan agreement with the debtor;*

- *Making management decisions for the debtor;*

- *Instructing the debtor which creditors should and should not be paid from available funds;*

- *Placing any of its employees as either a director or officer of the debtor;*

- *Influencing the removal from office of any of the debtor's personnel;*

- *Requesting that the debtor take any particular action at a shareholders meeting;*

- *Any involvement in handling the debtor's daily operations (no matter how innocuous); or*

- *Misleading other creditors to continue supplying the debtor with goods or services.*

Chapter 8

Thrown in the Bankruptcy Briar Patch

Our first case representing a client whose bank sold their loan to an investment fund was a simple, yet enormous, workout with a regional bank in trouble and liquidating loans as fast as possible. We had experience with this bank, which always helps, and we knew what to expect and how their processes worked. However, it turned out, that we didn't know what to expect at all.

The client received notice that its lender had sold its loans to an investment fund as part of a bulk transaction involving hundreds of loans. We had been in negotiation with the client's lender after the $31 million in loans matured. The bank demanded a large principal reduction and other terms that were unacceptable and financially impossible. The client was encouraged by the sale of the loans to investors; he hoped that the fund could better understand the difficulties of the current environment and work out an arrangement that benefited everyone. We soon knew better.

The collateral for the loans was four retail shopping centers. One was a "big box" retail center, and the other three were "non-anchored" and had no major tenant. The non-anchored shopping centers were profitable, but the company had completed the big box center near a resort community along the Gulf Coast as the economy sunk into a deep recession.

The original bank was worried about the big box center loan, which would be a huge loss, and also might sink the borrower's company. They did not want to let go of the profitable centers because they would lose their leverage in the negotiation of the fourth. The bank also believed that the parent company, being a large developer that owned dozens of commercial real estate projects, had the ability to borrow enough to cover the shortfall given time.

So they entered into a forbearance agreement with the borrower that extended the troubled big box loan but also cross-collateralized and cross-defaulted the loan with the loans on the three non-anchored centers. This was a serious mistake by the borrower in agreeing to such terms and ended up costing them over $500,000 in attorney's fees.

This was also a serious mistake by the original lender because they did not think about the potential effect this agreement would have on the borrower's bankruptcy reorganization options. Or they did know but decided to take their chances in order to call the loan performing for another quarter. Maybe, even knowing, they decided to take a chance that the hedge fund (which was buying a pool with hundreds of loans) would miss their mistake.

When a loan is sold to investors, rarely will the investor take a different approach than a bank lender. By and large investment funds hire former bankers to handle collections, so one would expect a similar approach.

And the bank's collection methods and strategies almost always work, remember? This fund was no exception. They rejected our proposals and expected payment in full, or they would file lawsuits and foreclose on the shopping centers.

Our objective was to place doubt in the mind of the asset manager and the fund. While expressing confidence in their legal case to us, behind closed doors they must have been worried. We made initial contact with the asset manager to provide an overview of the situation, but the fund replaced this asset manager shortly thereafter.

Research on the new asset manager revealed that he was one of the top executives in the fund. The fund was worried and bringing in the big guns.

Our first conference call must've had 20 participants, which amused us because neither our client nor their lawyers participated. Despite all of the people supposedly on this case, we realized a few things from this first call.

We learned that the fund, and also the original lender, did not understand how the corporate structure of the borrower would prevent collection of any deficiency. We also learned that the fund's asset managers did not understand the outcomes if the four shopping centers filed for bankruptcy reorganization. Third, and most important, we learned the "big gun" asset manager was a jackass.

The asset manager would scream at us that we had no case, and we'd calmly walk the whole crowd through exactly how the bankruptcy would be justified. We spelled out how the financial condition of the properties would justify approval of a plan of reorganization that would be unappetizing to the fund.

He boasted that a lawsuit was on the way that would crush the company, and they would collect every nickel owed. We responded that we'd be happy to provide contact information for the borrower's legal counsel to acknowledge the lawsuit. He threatened the guarantor—the parent company—with threats of a deep dive forensic audit of the company and its owners. We proposed having a meeting with the CFO and the company's accounting firm on whatever day was most convenient for them.

A graceful taunt is worth a thousand insults.

–Louis Nizer

When dealing with angry Type A personalities, responding in a calm and measured tone will make the person angrier, while screaming back at them will calm them down. This is similar to dealing with a bully who is emboldened by passive responses. We might engage in a shouting match so the guy on the other side can blow off steam.

In our case, making the asset manager as angry as possible made sense because he looked like a fool to the others from his company who were on the line, and also provided an opportunity to let the lender's counsel be the good guy. We knew that the case was going to court, and we knew that whoever the lawyers for the lender were, they wouldn't be angrier than the asset manager. Eventually this turned out to be exactly right, but we thought we were wrong at first.

Despite our explanation, the fund filed lawsuits and attempted to exercise its rental assignment. The company sought bankruptcy protection. Because the centers were in different locations and all owned by separate single-asset real estate entities, the lawyers had to file four separate bankruptcies in three different bankruptcy courts.

After an initial round of nasty tactical motions trying to force the client's law firm to recuse themselves, our side moved to consolidate the cases in one court, namely the court in which the parent company's principal place of business was located. The fund's first chance to torpedo the case was defeating this motion. Fortunately, the lawyers persuaded the judge that because the loans were cross-collateralized and cross-defaulted, the cases should be consolidated and treated as one credit.

Imagine the spectacle going on at this bankruptcy court hearing. The company's headquarters were in a rural part of the Deep South, and the bankruptcy court itself was in a small town. The New York hedge fund swarms in with a pack of Manhattan lawyers and their Midtown Atlanta local counsel to kick around the young CEO of the borrower. The CEO/owner is a success story in the community, the son of a politician legendary in the area, and an employer of hundreds in the local hotel and retail industries. Federal judges may be appointed for life, but they still want to play golf at the local country club and don't like eating alone. Not to say that there was any "home cooking" on this case, but the optics for the fund were absolutely the worst (not that we needed any "home cooking;" if we thought we had to rely on that kind of tactic to win the bankruptcy case, we wouldn't have filed in the first place).

Winning this motion was essential to the borrower's case because as consolidated, the borrower could argue that because the equity in the three performing centers exceeded the deficiency in the fourth,[10] the debtor entities had equity in the project as well as positive cash flow, which are essential elements to prevail against the fund's inevitable motion to dismiss the bankruptcy case(s).

The borrower was also able to prevail on its motion to control cash collateral, meaning that the fund could not exercise its rental assignment and force the tenants to pay the fund directly instead of paying the management company as required by the leases. Because the borrower prevailed on this motion, the centers would continue to operate, which was important because it enabled the borrower to dig in for a long war.

Exactly as we had explained in the conference call nine months previously, our client was able to prevail on all of the key motions in bankruptcy court. Through negotiation, we were able to demonstrate to the fund that because of the unique corporate structure and the nature of their investment in all of its projects, a judgment would be unlikely if not impossible to collect against the parent company. With approval of a reorganization plan a virtual certainty, the fund agreed to dismiss the lawsuits, accept a significantly discounted payoff amount, and allow the company 18 months to source the necessary funding for the discounted payoff.

The client was satisfied with the outcome and learned that the investment funds who purchase loans from banks, particularly the large players who buy in billion dollar blocks, will typically take the same approach to collection as the banks.

*   *   *   *   *

---

[10] "*Arguing they have equity in the consolidated projects? Doesn't that contradict what was said earlier, namely that the fund couldn't collect on any deficiency? If the loan has a collateral deficiency, then by definition there's not equity, correct?*"
Ah, but note the borrower *could argue* they had equity. A funny thing about bankruptcy is the debtor and creditors' opinions on the value of the collateral take a 180-degree turn. Now the debtor wants to prove there isn't a deficiency because if it doesn't, they lose. The creditor then naturally changes its position to argue the value is lower.
The judge in this cases wanted no part of the fund's argument that, before bankruptcy, we argued the properties' value was much lower than the loan balances. The judge understood both parties were posturing in the negotiation, and a fight over the appraisals would settle the matter.

In our experience, most banks don't think about their actual recovery net of expenses. The asset manager simply wants to get the highest settlement number possible.

A few banks, and most hedge funds, look at their recovery net of expenses, which helps on rare occasions but not often. This is because the loan purchaser takes collections expenses into account when determining the value of the loan and negotiating the purchase price of the loan from the lender. They are also seeking to maximize their recovery through the traditional collections methods, but they are seeking a target rate of return, whereas the original lender would be trying to minimize losses.

A simple example: Fund buys a $100 loan from Bank at 50 cents on the dollar, and the fund's target return is 20 percent. They are counting on collecting $60 net of expenses and may not take ANY deal below that. Why? Because it's easier for the asset manager guy to explain to his boss that they couldn't hit the number and therefore had to foreclose on the asset at $25. Management is used to this scenario. "We squeezed the borrower, but he couldn't come up with enough cash. We had to foreclose," is easy to explain.

But even if the borrower could source $45 to pay off the loan, if the asset manager takes that deal he is going to get his ass chewed by management because he lost the investors' money. This is unacceptable—you are fired!

Um, excuse me, but in the first scenario didn't the fund lose more money than it lost in the second scenario?

This is why you don't run a hedge fund. The fund has a budget for foreclosure losses. They've taken foreclosure losses into account in the fund's offering documents. The investors knew that could happen. Settling with the borrower for a lower recovery than the $60 target is unacceptable, and under $50 unforgivable, because there isn't a budget for that.

This is a bit of an exaggeration (just a little bit), but this is how it goes. Everybody knows that losses happen when making a risky investment. But *unexpected* losses, *unanticipated* losses, will get an asset manager *fired* and his asset management company crossed off the list when the private equity people are handing out loan packages from their next $1 billion loan purchase.

The fun part (actually, not fun) for the borrower is that, while all of that is going on, you have no idea what their target number is, no idea what the discounted price was the fund paid, and no idea what the fund can or cannot do to dispose of the loan. The borrower has to treat the workout as with an ordinary bank in almost every circumstance.

Unfortunately for borrowers, courts have ruled a loan buyer/assignee has no obligation whatsoever to the borrower to disclose anything—unless required by the loan documents. An originating lender would never agree to a provision in the loan documents that a successor-assignee of the loan disclose such information. If the originating bank did, they could never sell the loan—nobody would buy it, or the buyer would discount the value too low for the selling bank to sell it.

Note Buying for Fun, Profit and Revenge

July, 2009

A man loaned his neighbor a large amount of cash on a handshake to help bail out a real estate deal. When it became evident that he wasn't going to be paid back, his lawyer correctly advised him that he would be considered an unsecured creditor in a lawsuit or judgment, and that he was better off trying to work this out. He could not get the neighbor to pay him, so he came to us. "What can you do?"

The neighbor knew he had our client over a barrel because our client's loan was unsecured. As we researched public records on the neighbor, we learned that he had a good number of income-producing properties, and one of his loans was for sale by his bank. This was an opportunity to transform our client's loan.

Careful review of the security documents for the loan to be auctioned revealed that the loan agreement contained a "dragnet clause," a provision wherein the borrower agrees that the collateral is security for the subject loan, but also any other obligation of the borrower to the lender. If our client purchases the loan, he would step into the shoes of the neighbor's real estate lender, and the collateral for the auctioned loan would become collateral for his handshake deal as well.

The client bought that loan and we notified the neighbor that at maturity, which was about six months away, we expected payment in full on both loans. When at maturity the neighbor did not pay, the client filed a lawsuit. The court denied the borrower's motion arguing that the handshake loan wasn't secured by the purchased loan.

We entered into a seven-month long process in court, moving through discovery and various hearings. We eventually worked out a settlement. The borrower fully performed and paid the settlement, and our client eventually recovered all of his principal and the amount he paid for the loan. He also learned the lesson everyone eventually learns about handshake deals. His neighbor learned a lesson, too:

Don't mess with a man who will risk $800,000 to collect $75,000.

The dragnet clause is one of those provisions tucked into the "boilerplate" miscellaneous provisions at the end of the document that can wreak havoc on a borrower's life. When reviewing loan documents for the first time, we go to the boilerplate first. Checking for dragnet clauses, lender's right of set-off (meaning the bank can empty your bank accounts with them if you default on a loan), choice of law (what state law applies?), venue (in which jurisdiction must the lender sue the borrower, and can we remove the case from state to federal court?), and amendment provisions (did the lender follow its own procedures in amending the documents?) to name a few. These provisions can sometimes be the borrower's get out of jail free card and other times be a ticking time bomb.

Chapter 9

"It's not you. It's me."

This Loan Must Go—lender withdraws from the marketplace.

An attorney referred a client to us; they were partners in a successful professional recruiting business. When times were good, their business was expanding to the point they needed a line of credit to fund growth. But when bad times hit, their company's business was particularly vulnerable, and all of their profit disappeared overnight. Their line of credit wasn't renewed, and they did not have cash to pay it off. The bank sent a letter demanding payment and threatening a lawsuit if they weren't paid.

The client had the ability to keep making payments on the loan, and possibly even pay off the loan in full given a little bit of time. But the bank was not interested in negotiating and filed its lawsuit.

This bank's asset manager was particularly uncooperative, so we welcomed the possibility of a lawsuit to put distance between the bank and the borrower. Prior to our involvement, the direct contact between the parties turned ugly, early. A lawsuit might allow cooler heads to prevail.

The borrowers could have even sourced a hard money loan or "vulture capital" to pay the bank in full, but they did not want to go that route; the interest rate and collateral requirements were too high for them. They'd take their chances in court. If the bank won the lawsuit, they would be able to collect because the client had no asset protection plans in place.

Despite the acrimony and the bank's advantageous position in litigation, the bank accepted our offer to settle the loan for a discounted payoff of about 70 percent of the loan balance. We were sure that if we could offer a fairly decent number, the bank would take it to get paid now rather than spend more money on lawyers and collection expenses. How did we know this?

In our background research on this particular lender, we discovered that the bank was now owned by an out-of-state bank that had acquired our client's bank at the peak of the market and had lost tens of millions of dollars on bad loans. The out-of-state bank was winding up operations and leaving the state.

This meant all of the loans had to go. They were not interested in relationships. It also explains why, prior to our involvement, the lender had been particularly aggressive, nasty and intimidating (which only made it harder to get our own client to come to the table). They did not care about burning bridges. We knew they were not interested in continuing business in this state and were looking to cut their losses. We gave the bank an easy route to cross another loan off the list and move on to the next one.

This couple realized that their business does well when times are good but can be in great danger when times are bad if they don't plan for the worst. They operate the company debt free and are doing better than ever.

Sometimes a bank can't afford to do a deal that makes sense because of financial difficulties.

By far the most difficult lender to work with is a bank that cannot afford to do a deal that makes sense because of its own financial problems. You must obtain and review the most recent FDIC "call report" for the bank with whom you are dealing.[11]

---

[11] Call reports are available at this address:
https://cdr.ffiec.gov/public/ManageFacsimiles.aspx.

Look for a high Texas Ratio.[12] Any ratio over 100 (i.e., 1:1) means the bank is suffering considerable difficulty with problem loans. A bank with a Texas Ratio over 200 will not be able to make a settlement if the loan needs to be settled at a significant loss. The bank has a better chance of failing than surviving.

As the economy has recovered, most banks that did not fail have recovered along with it, and those banks still in financial trouble get by with "creative accounting" techniques and a dash of regulatory willful blindness. However, examining any public information on the adversary can yield important information.

When the housing market fell apart, a residential developer approached us. He was struggling with a residential construction project, which was only half built when the housing market crashed. He continued to make all loan payments out of his own pocket even after his partner went bankrupt and disengaged. His lender would only do 60-day renewals (to avoid having the site re-appraised), raised his interest rate, and charged a small origination fee every time.

After several of those renewals, he demanded a longer-term renewal. They told him no. Our mission was to either negotiate a three-year renewal on acceptable terms or convince the bank to agree to a discounted payoff.

This client had significant cash assets, the mortgage was paid off on his personal residence, and he owned a number of residential rental properties debt free. He had always borrowed money carefully and had been conservative, never borrowing money if he did not have a sure way to pay off. He went to great lengths to maintain the values of the homes in the neighborhood development, and was responsible with the way he spent money.

Initially, the lender was stubborn and contentious in negotiations. When we refused to sign another 60-day renewal, the lender filed a lawsuit against our client personally. They sought a judgment against him on the personal

---

[12] "The **Texas ratio** takes the amount of a bank's non-performing assets and loans, as well as loans delinquent for more than 90 days, and divides this number by the firm's tangible capital equity plus its loan loss reserve." –definition from Investopedia

guarantee because they did not want to foreclose on the lots. He engaged a lawyer who responded to the lawsuit.

Meanwhile, we met with the bank and explained our proposals to them, all of which the bank rejected. Our client was in a vulnerable position because of his unencumbered assets and plenty of liquidity. He would be in big trouble if the bank obtained a judgment against him personally. We identified cash and liquid assets to contribute, and secured a line of credit (which was extremely challenging given the pending litigation) such that, if a bank judgment was unavoidable, he would wave the white flag and pay off the bank's loan. In doing so he would be in a precarious position with the line of credit he had, but that would be the lesser of two evils. The new line of credit also gave him flexibility in the short term because he could continue to fund an expensive, protracted fight with the lender.

We were prepared to take this one the distance, but we were surprised, after several months of litigation, when the bank's lawyer informed us that the bank would offer to settle the case if the borrower could come up with a lump sum cash payment of 65 cents on the dollar by the end of the month. This made no sense and was a 180-degree shift of position.

Looking at the calendar, we noticed that the end of the month was also the end of the quarter. This was a case of a lender's own financial issues driving the process. The bank was a small community bank, and this loan was one of their largest loans. They were carrying this large loan on its balance sheet as a performing loan, even though the decline in value of the property (undeveloped lots) put the loan deeply underwater.

The bank has a method to the 60-day extension madness. If a bank extends a loan term, the extension is a de facto refinance, which regulations require that the bank re-appraise the collateral. But a short-term extension is excepted from this rule to extend a maturity date if circumstances warrant, e.g., the borrower's sale/refinance transaction is delayed past the maturity date. If a bank knows the loan is underwater but doesn't want to classify it as distressed (which requires them to reserve capital to cover the potential loss), it can give the short extensions and rely on the old appraisal done before the collateral's value declined.

If the property were reappraised, they would have to move it to non-performing status and commit precious reserves against the loan, which would hurt the bank's financial reports. When the lender decided that it no choice but to file a lawsuit, the loan immediately had to be classified non-performing in the next call report.

We agreed to the payment amount and closed the settlement on the last day of the quarter. Our client settled the lawsuit, retained the property, and was relieved of any liability for the remainder of the loan. While allowing our client to keep his property, the settlement enabled the bank to dispose of a large problem loan while adding cash to its balance sheet.

Money Center Banks

Money center banks (Bank of America, Wells Fargo, Citi, JP Morgan Chase, et al.) have more flexibility to accomplish favorable settlements. The reasons should be obvious: an endless supply of cash, the backstop of the Federal Reserve, and the moral hazard both create.[13] "Too big to fail, and too big to jail." Money center banks can often take enormous losses with impunity. But it takes the right asset manager, good timing, and a little luck. One of our clients owned a successful small business, and in the good times they took out

---

[13] *"Global history records governments of all political persuasions using taxpayer funds to support distressed institutions. As undesirable as it may be to put taxpayer funds at risk to support financial institutions, in the midst of a crisis it is often the fastest and most certain option to stabilise the system and avoid widespread economic damage.*
Investors can rationally surmise that the government is likely to rescue systemically important institutions if no other options exist, as their collapse would cause the most damage to the financial system and broader economy. This leads to a belief that some institutions are too-big-to-fail — that they receive an implicit government guarantee. Perceptions of this implicit guarantee have costs. A government may need to rescue a troubled institution in a crisis, putting taxpayer funds at risk. It may also cause 'moral hazard'. This means it may encourage systemically important institutions to take on more risk than is optimal, since they believe they receive any benefits from the risk taking while the government will bear the cost of failure. Further, investors may believe they will not make a loss, even if the institution fails, so they have less incentive to monitor the institution's risks and apply market discipline. This can lead to a lower cost of funding for these institutions.[11] Any lower funding costs might allow the institutions to become larger and more systemically important. The overall system can therefore become larger than is economically efficient, exacerbating the size of the potential cost of a crisis and therefore the size of the perceived guarantee." –Source: Interim Report of the Financial System Inquiry (Australia), 2014

a large, even for them, loan on a condominium they bought at a beach resort that would become one of the most spectacular real estate failures ever.

In this case, we coached the borrower because it was a *de facto* consumer loan. In those situations, it's mostly filling out forms the right way.[14] The bank settled the condominium loan for 15 cents on the dollar.

One contributing factor was that their condo was the last in the whole resort upon which the lender had not already foreclosed. The bank already knew that their collateral was worthless, and this particular property was in a judicial foreclosure state, which means the foreclosure would be expensive and time consuming. Furthermore, the state had passed various consumer protection laws, which made obtaining a judgment against a consumer borrower on a deficiency more difficult.

Most of our client's assets were income producing real estate, encumbered by debt, but they had equity and cash flow. Their business had recovered somewhat from the Great Recession. However, the bank decided that spending years in court trying to collect would not be worth the trouble. This project failed, and our clients, who had never missed a payment, were the last ones standing. Settling enabled the bank to close the book on a disastrous project and start anew. The clients were lucky in a sense. This was a bad investment, but luckily it was *so bad* that its condition influenced the lender in a favorable way.

---

[14] We do not ordinarily advise clients on consumer loans, but we did in this case because we also worked out the client's business loans.

Chapter 10

"Your 17% rate is actually 60%."

Government-Guaranteed Debts

With government-guaranteed loans, be ready for additional thick, tough layers of bureaucracy, which you must penetrate efficiently to accomplish a settlement.

August, 2013

This case was unique in that a lender referred us. The banker called us about one of his borrowers, who owed his bank several million dollars. The borrower had a successful operating company with multiple locations over a large territory. His business had a predictable flow of income. When his loans started maturing, the client and his banker realized that in reality, the whole operation was on the verge of collapse.

We were hired to negotiate with the company's other creditors, so the biggest creditor—our banker friend—wouldn't be forced to shut down the company and take a huge loss on its loans. Unfortunately for the company, its business was very sensitive to one thing nobody can control, namely the weather. About the time many loans matured, the weather was bad for months on end. Revenue plummeted, and profits became losses. This made it impossible to find takeout financing for any of the loans.

Analyzing the company's financial situation, we discovered that only a few of the company's locations were profitable. Among its many loans were real estate loans with guarantees from the federal Small Business Association (SBA), and these locations were worth far less than the loan balances: the company needed to shut them down. The loans would need to be settled if the company were to survive.

In our discussions with the lender, we had to explain that their properties were in a unique situation. One was worthless as a location and was costing the company less by sitting dark—the store had been closed for months. The other location had certain leased equipment installed that were not fixtures—they were not collateral for the loan.

The equipment was essential for the business. This was also significant in that the equipment lessor was not bound by its lease to honor successors-in-interest, such as a foreclosing bank or a purchaser. We told the bank that if they foreclosed, the lessor would remove the equipment. This would be perfectly legal and render the location worthless to anyone; the property would become a bank-owned "tear down."

We negotiated a settlement of the loans in question at approximately 40 cents on the dollar. We assisted the client and its accountant with preparing the appropriate documentation, known as an "Offer in Compromise." Thanks to the settlement, the company was able to drastically improve its cash flow, stay in business, and keep our banker friend's loans performing on the profitable locations.

In an SBA guarantee situation, the relationship between you and the lender changes. Yes, the lender will drive a hard bargain and negotiate aggressively, but in the end, the lender must get approval from the appropriate government agency to settle a defaulted loan.

The lender, when they agree to a settlement with a borrower, becomes an advocate. They are your advocate because if the SBA accepts the Offer in Compromise, the SBA pays the bank for any deficiency in excess of 10 percent. For instance, if a bank has a defaulted $1 million SBA loan and is only able to collect $500,000 from the borrower, the SBA guarantee would reimburse the bank $400,000. These programs are hugely popular with smaller banks because the terms are reasonable for the borrowers, and a huge secondary market exists into which they can quickly sell the loans to investment funds, insurance companies, and pensions.

The lender must recommend the settlement to the SBA and argue on the borrower's behalf that the settlement is the best recovery for everyone. As with all government programs, the process is forms-driven. The bank, not the borrower, submits the forms and supporting documentation to the government guarantor and argues for approval. Loans guaranteed by the U.S. Department of Agriculture and other federal loan guarantee programs have a process similar to SBA loans.

Negotiating any loan with a guarantee from a government entity (including many types of bonds) requires a different approach with the lender than a "normal" loan default situation. Being cooperative from the start is essential, because your enemy will soon be your advocate to the SBA.

Specialty Finance Companies

We consider the term Specialty Finance Companies to mean lenders who lend primarily against assets with high collateral coverage (i.e., low loan-to-value) and high interest rates. Factoring and merchant advance loans are good examples, and oftentimes the transaction is structured to disguise the true cost of capital.

Companies with cash flow, particularly small businesses, are the primary targets for these types of financing. This client's story is a classic case of trying to solve debt problems by borrowing more money.

October, 2013

A convenience store business with multiple locations, which were mostly owned and mortgaged, had large debt service payments plus its operating costs. The company had been profitable through the Great Recession, but in 2012, the company's CFO went on an unplanned medical leave of absence and wasn't replaced. Cash flow cratered. The lack of financial control seriously impacted revenues and exposed many operational weaknesses that were unknown or safely ignored when the company was profitable.

Desperate for cash to cover debt payments, the company took out "merchant advance" loans on the credit card receivables at its two most profitable stores, which kept most of the other debt payments current for a time. But the merchant advance loans' cost was killing the company's cash flow, which eventually led the mortgages back into default. For the company to survive, the merchant advance loans needed to go—and at a discount.

With these loans, borrowers get quick cash. The transaction can close in days and is structured not as a loan, but as an asset purchase. The "asset" is certain of the company's "future receivables," meaning a percentage of credit card payments made, every day, until the lender collects the "stated amount," meaning the payoff balance. The transaction is structured this way to avoid state usury laws, because while the borrower believes they are paying interest in the mid-teens, the real return for the lender is 50 to 60 percent, sometimes even higher.

For instance, the lender loans $400, and the borrower must pay back $460 via a daily draw by the lender of 17 percent of its credit card receipts. The loan has no maturity date, and if the borrower goes out of business, all of the outstanding balance is forgiven. If the borrower did this loan once, it might not be bad. But after the first loan is made, the lender is constantly offering more money that can be sent to the borrower in one or two days, and many borrowers find the offer irresistible. In many instances, the borrower has an incentive to borrow more under this arrangement because the business has cash flow problems caused by the loan itself.

How does a 17 percent payment yield 60 percent interest? Time. The lender underwrites the borrower's credit card receivables and derives the loan payoff amount, and the daily percentage by assuming the receipts will pay of the loan in three or four months. In our example, if the borrower pays off the $460 in three months, the lender's annualized return is 60 percent. These are uncomfortable discussions to have with borrowers who think they are paying 17 percent and are actually paying 60 percent.

And on top of that, the lender often requires the borrower to use the lender's captive credit card processing company. The lender gets its share of those fees, and the borrower has agreed to allow the lender to ACH out of the operating account, every day.

In our case, thanks to a cooperative bank, we were able to close the associated accounts and stop paying, while making a smooth transition to new operating accounts. The merchant advance lender was not pleased. However, we did reach a settlement after several months of back-and-forth.

We discovered that one of the locations was only barely profitable, so the borrower closed the location and paid the lender a nominal amount. The lender settled the loan on the second location at 40 cents on the dollar after we painted the financial picture: all of the company's properties were security for other loans, and the guarantor owned few unsecured assets of value other than the business itself. The possibility of the lender collecting on a judgment was remote.

Altogether the borrower received around a 75 percent discount on the loan payoff, but even so, the lender still sported a nearly 50 percent return on its loan. Settling those merchant advance loans, closing unprofitable locations, and improving operations enable the company to service its debt and survive the crisis.

Chapter 11

The Private Equity Strip Out

*A man who has never gone to school may
steal from a freight car; but if he has a university
education, he may steal the whole railroad.*

–Theodore Roosevelt

Restructuring debt for an operating business can differ greatly from real estate debt; each type requires a different kind of strategy to achieve results. With an operating business as borrower, the liquidation value of the collateral is usually far less than a real estate loan. Furniture, fixtures, equipment, and machinery in a liquidation mode usually have little value that the lender can recover after fees and sales cost. The collateral is worth far more to the operating business, and worth more in use by the operating business, than the collateral is worth on the auction floor.

If the borrower's business is down but can produce an operating profit before debt service, then bankruptcy reorganization is a distinct possibility. If the business is not generating enough operating profits, then we have to identify what operational problems are causing the profitability decline. As the borrower restructures its operations, educate the lender about problems with operations and how the lenders should restructure the borrower's debt.

The borrower's ultimate goal is always debt forgiveness, the discounted payoff. A discounted payoff is highly unlikely unless unforeseen factors come into play in the situation (or brought into the situation).

September, 2011

An operating company manufactures parts and machinery sold to large multinational corporations. The company generates healthy operating profits and had no difficulty covering debt service. The company's business relies on a line of credit from a super-regional bank. Even though the borrower never missed a loan payment, the bank kept shrinking their lines of credit, which was not acceptable for operating a business of this nature. The bank wanted to force the company into bankruptcy and liquidate the assets because the bank erroneously believed that the assets had sufficient value to pay off the loan in full.

Prior to the bank shrinking their lines of credit, this company was profitable, generating a little over $1 million in net profit every year. A small private equity group bought a controlling interest in the company via a leveraged buyout and did what private equity groups do: they borrowed as much as possible against the assets and cash flow, and pulled out all of the cash.

Unfortunately, the private equity group that owned the company took the position that they would not invest any more money in the company. They had made a good profit on their investment and didn't care if the business died. Anything they could get from liquidating the company was gravy.

The way this manufacturing company operated, they signed contracts, and received progress payments as they build the equipment, but the company used its multimillion-dollar line of credit to fund payroll, materials, etc., while they awaited payment from the large, mostly overseas, corporations. Being large multinational manufacturers, they took their time paying. In our experience, no amount of persuasion can convince these mega-corporations to more promptly turn around accounts payable, even though the downside for them was considerable: the company produced custom-made parts for use in robotic manufacturing machinery.

Importantly, the loan required a cash collection "lockbox." All the cash that came in went to the bank's lockbox account, and the bank applied the funds first to the line of credit. Every week company management had to beg the bank to fund payroll and other items. One week, the bank refused to fund the payroll because they reduced the line of credit, which left the entity no choice but to file for reorganization and move for control of cash, which the judge granted. This allowed them to pay payroll and operate.

The bank's attempt to control its own balance sheet by reducing lines of credit could result in putting a very profitable company out of business. This was a super-regional bank in financial trouble, and they had two reasons for killing this profitable company.

First, the regulators had restricted credit guidelines such that the bank had to reduce the borrowing base for the company's receivables. At the time, the bank would not lend as much on cash flow because of the uncertainty in the economy, and discounted the receivables as collateral to the point that the company did not have enough credit to cover its own payroll, let alone the other operating expenses.

Second, the regulators had increased bank capitalization requirements, i.e., the ratio of the bank's capital to the bank's total outstanding credit issued. Because the bank was in trouble, they were unable to raise capital (i.e., the numerator). The only way left to improve the ratio was to lower the denominator. And the easiest way to lower the amount of outstanding credit is to cut operating lines of credit. These loans typically renew annually, and the borrower is at the mercy of their lender if the borrower cannot obtain credit elsewhere.

When a business is dependent on an operating line of credit that renews annually, prepare contingency plans to operate if the line is cut, or not renewed at all. This would include preparing for reorganization.

The company management, who were the original owners of the company, was desperate to save it. Our plan was to have an investor buy the line of credit from that bank. However, we knew that the investor would not agree to purchase the loan unless the bank agreed to sell at a significant discount.

The *coup de grâce* was the company filing for bankruptcy, which meant that with no potential purchasers of the company as an operating business, the loan would trade at or below the estimated value of the assets at liquidation. Through negotiation and presenting a persuasive case as to the liquidation value of the company assets, we eventually persuaded the bank to agree to have our investor buy the line of credit for 60 cents on the dollar. By providing expert opinions and backup documentation demonstrating that the value of pieces of equipment of this type was little more than scrap metal value, we were able to convince them that taking a discounted payoff made sense for them.

Although the bank was in trouble, it had shrunk the line of credit to the point where the real discount amount was not unacceptably large. Furthermore, because the bank had forced the company into distress and default, they had designated the loan as "distressed" and discounted the value of the loan on their books to a number, obviously, less than 60 percent of the outstanding balance.

What was important about buying the loan of a bankrupt company? The management wanted the company they built to survive, and if they sourced a friendly investor partner to purchase the loan, we would control the senior debt. This put our investor in a position to negotiate a fairly inexpensive buyout of the private equity group. The private equity guys held a controlling interest in the company, but if the minority interest holders in the company (i.e., the former owners) controlled the senior debt, they could foreclose on the assets. Such an outcome would wipe out everyone's equity, and the investor would own everything.

This made negotiating a buyout of the private equity group easy. Their choices were (a) do nothing and get nothing, (b) continue the bankruptcy and present a reorganization plan for approval, which they didn't want to do, or (c) take a nominal payment for their worthless ownership interest and get out, to which they agreed. The investor would purchase their interest for a nominal amount and fund the discounted payoff of the line of credit.

As part of the deal between the investor and company management, the investor agreed that the company management and the investor would create a new entity wherein the friendly investor held the controlling ownership interest, company management would own a minority interest and keep their jobs. The company could continue operating with no debt service, which would enable them to fund operations without a line of credit. With their strong balance sheet and solid, though slow-paying, receivables, they could also obtain a line of credit from a new lender.

This case ended badly. The investor was inexperienced and attempted to renegotiate the deal at the last minute, and the deal fell apart. Everyone lost. The bank refused to take less than 60 cents on the dollar, foreclosed, and liquidated the company. The liquidation yielded 12 cents on the dollar, so the loss on the loan was more than doubled even before the expenses in bankruptcy and liquidation. The bank's outcome was more than a total loss.

The owners of the company lost all of their investments in cash, sweat, and stress. An operating company with $1 million in annual profits went down the drain. All of the employees lost their jobs. The company's customers lost a valuable supplier and had to scramble to find replacements, which led to production delays, lost profits, etc.

The investor lost all of the transaction costs and what would've been double-digit returns on its money, and as the company's industry came roaring back to life in the mid-2010s, the company could have obtained a new bank loan and paid off the investor with a 67 percent capital gain inside of three years.

Everyone lost as the deal fell apart. Big time. Except the private equity investors. When they ran up the company's debt to strip-out the cash, the loans returned their invested capital, and they pocketed a handsome return from their equity position in the company before it imploded.

Part 3

"I know of no higher fortitude than stubbornness in the face of overwhelming odds."

–Louis Nizer

Chapter 12

Negotiating with Inferior Bargaining Power

Entrepreneurs look at economic risk as an opportunity. Business people make a decision by asking, "What's going to cost me the least amount of money? What is going to maximize my return? How can I close this deal quickly and move on to new opportunities?" When a borrower can't service, refinance, or satisfy its debts, the borrower has a problem. But the creditors may also have a problem, which creates such an opportunity.

Banks, other creditors, regulators and the like always focus more on the risk than the opportunity. This is a primary reason entrepreneurs are not well suited for negotiating disputes in these situations.[15]

---

[15] If you are skeptical of this statement, consider this: entrepreneurs evaluate a situation by deciding "am I willing and able to absorb the loss this risk would cause if it happened?" If the answer is yes, the risk is worth it. If the answer is no, then a deal never happens.

The decision making process with banks and most other lenders is very slow. Banks make every decision by committee, and a more senior committee or a C-level executive may have to approve the committee's decision. The process is long and drawn out; patience is immensely important. And the negotiation happens on an ever-changing landscape. Nothing can be done to speed up the process except accepting an unfavorable outcome.

Debt collectors know that entrepreneurs get impatient, and if they reveal a sense of urgency, the collector will often slow progress to a crawl and, very often, the debtor will come up with more money.

Both sides will try hard to get the best possible deal, but you see the disconnect: the borrower's primary goal is to make the best deal possible as quickly as possible. The lender's primary goal is to follow procedure, which can be governing documents of a fund and FDIC regulations for a bank, as well as other laws, regulations, and internal procedures the company must follow. Whatever the outcome, it must be inside the box.

How do we bridge this gap and get a favorable outcome different from what the lender expects and demands? First we must eliminate all other alternatives. Optimally, we would make the lender believe our preferred alternative was their idea. To accomplish this, we unfortunately must do all of the work for them.

To get approval from a committee, the asset manager has to (a) clearly explain the proposal, and (b) understand why the other, usual alternatives will not work. For this to happen, the borrower's side will need to provide all of the information and a written description of the deal for the asset manager to present.

Meanwhile, if a large bureaucratic organization assumes a risk that does not come to pass, this is considered business as usual. If everything works out fine, the lender is paid in full and on time, the loan officer did his job, i.e., they accomplished what management expected of them. But if something *does* go wrong, the customer breaches its agreements, and the risk comes to pass, or the loan officer didn't evaluate the risk properly in the first place, somebody's ass is getting chewed and booted out the door.

In debtor/creditor disputes or business divorce, the bureaucracy tries to impose an unacceptable risk upon the entrepreneur, and the entrepreneur cannot walk away. This is very stressful for the entrepreneur because, as we previously explained, entrepreneurs tend to be conflict averse. And stress leads to an irrational assessment of the situation (and the risks, for that matter), which leads to bad decision-making.

More importantly, the asset manager's job doesn't depend upon resolving your case, and the only way your case could cost the asset manager his job is if he agrees to something like what you propose. This is why you must close off all other possible alternatives.

You close off all other alternatives via the thrust and parry with the lender's collection efforts, while at the same time painting the accurate financial picture for the lender to demonstrate why their proposals/demands can't be met or shouldn't be met. The process can be maddening because we wait for the lender to act while at the same time negotiating against ourselves.

Negotiating with a bank (and most other creditors) is negotiating against yourself, and you must acclimate yourself to this fact.

A bank may make offers, but the offers are always the same offer rearranged to look like a different offer. Beware of proposals in which the borrower agrees to make payments or take other action, and in exchange the lender will "consider'" taking favorable action.

Oftentimes this arises as "if the borrower will agree to make monthly payments for nine months, and all payments are made on time, the bank will 'consider' a three-year renewal..."

Many borrowers will unwittingly agree to this because the special assets loan officer repeatedly assures the borrower that this is all the regulations permit the bank to do, but that the renewal is all but guaranteed and standard operating procedure. They can't write it down that way, etc. Nine payments later the bank "considers" the renewal and decides that, "Yes, Mr. Borrower, we have considered an extension and will agree to do so, but you need to make an additional payment of $50,000 and the extension can only be for 12 months," etc., etc. This negotiation tactic is common and surprisingly effective.

We prefer to not call out the other side on their obvious gamesmanship, but to gamesmanly rearrange our own offer to be essentially the same thing but stated differently. This technique, delivered with a straight face, delivers the "stop fooling around" message in a non-insulting way and dispenses with any more idiotic, deckchair-rearranging proposals.

Bank kicks can down road. A $10 million mistake.

July, 2010

A money center bank loaned our clients tens of millions of dollars on three real estate projects. Two of the projects were big successes. One was a profitable hotel rated as one of the top performers in the country among its brand, and another project was a triple-net real estate lease to one of America's best-known retailers.

The third project was not so lucky. Everything about the project was wrong; the wrong type of project in the wrong location at precisely the wrong time. It was deeply underwater. Our client's problem was that it looked like the bad project was going to cause them to lose the two home runs.

One year earlier, the lender and client agreed to an extension agreement on the failing project. The asset manager demanded that the borrower protect the bank's position by agreeing to cross default and cross collateralize the two performing projects with the troubled deal. The parent company, which guaranteed all three loans, agreed. This was a mistake by both parties.

We could never emphasize this point enough:

Never give additional collateral in exchange for short-term extensions.

The borrower made a mistake because his money-making, home run deals were ensnared in a loan $10 million underwater, and because the company did not have access to that much cash, they might be forced to sell their performing locations under duress, for far less than they were worth, give the money to the bank, and lose two great income streams. We have seen this result far, far too often.

The bank also made a mistake. In attempting to "dress up the pig" by rolling it into a bigger portfolio, which taken in the aggregate they could consider 'performing,' they lost the ability to settle the bad loan by itself.

Because the extension had ended, the parent company was in default on $25 million, and thus ALL of the loans had to go.

After over a year of negotiation, the bank agreed to allow the company to sell the failed project to a vulture investor at a considerable loss. Because we were able to demonstrate to the asset manager that this recovery was the best they could hope for given the changes in the economy and the condition of the parent company, the bank forgave an almost $10 million deficiency. The two performing projects were refinanced in part with new bank debt, and a small equity injection by the company's partners completed the payoff.

The bank, hopefully, after taking a substantial loss, learned that cross-collateralizing does not work unless the failing project has a chance to recover. After going through two years of real danger of bankruptcy, hopefully our client learned that extend-and-pretend forbearance agreements are dangerous unless you have a real exit strategy planned out in advance. You must carefully assess the economics and unintended consequences before agreeing to extension and forbearance agreements. If the reason for agreeing is to kick the can down the road, you may lose a good project by trying to save a bad project that never had a chance.

In some instances, a creditor will make an initial offer early in the process that is only slightly less than the full amount owed. Treat this initial proposal as the 'payment in full' demand. If slightly discounted, the creditor's offer is only to discount a portion of fees, interest, attorney's fees or the like, which the bank may be entitled in the loan documents. Such a proposal is a collections tactic to appear reasonable and cooperative, when in reality the proposal is only gouging the debtor slightly less.

Usually the lender will not make an offer for less than payment in full for many months, if not years. A measure of fatigue must first take hold on their side. Time has passed; money spent; none collected. Offering to accept less than the full amount owed is a significant milestone in the process. It is "the end of the beginning."

"Now this is not the end. It is not even the beginning of the end. But it is, perhaps, the end of the beginning." – Winston Churchill, after the decisive

defeat of the Axis armies in North Africa at the Battle of El Alamein, November, 1942

When the bank, lender, creditor, plaintiff, etc., offers to take less than the full amount claimed, the case is no longer about "justice." We are just arguing about a number. We may argue for many more months or years, but the lender's posture must necessarily soften, which is why it takes such a long time to get there in the first place.

On Ambiguity

One thing we must teach clients is to live within ambiguity and uncertainty and learn to appreciate both of them. Both sides have uncertainties in the case, both real and imagined, known or unknown. The entire process is cloaked in ambiguity.

Everything coming from the lender is ambiguous by definition because the special assets officer with whom you are dealing not only has no authority to bind the lender to anything, and he/she probably isn't a good communicator. But as we will discuss later, the nature of the negotiation makes the other side's ambiguity nothing compared to *our* ambiguity.

Our ambiguity is key. We can be ambiguous, and the other side probably won't even notice. Why? Because people interpret what you say as being what they want to hear. And if the other side notices ambiguity, they still don't ask the right questions. Why? Because not only do people hear what they want to hear, they assume they know the answers to the questions they ask.

> *"If they can get you asking the wrong questions,*
> *they don't have to worry about answers."*
>
> – Thomas Pynchon

In rare instances, the other side may swerve into the right questions—the questions that collections specialists know to ask, or forensic accountants, or fraud investigators. These types of people usually aren't doing loan workouts for lenders. When confronted with questions about ambiguity by design, always be prepared with the correct answer. But this rarely happens. If you can put a certain spin on the answer, great. If not, tell the truth and move back to the next line of defense. Repeat as necessary.

The lender's attitude changes over the course of the process. In the beginning you would think the money owed belonged to the asset manager himself, and he considers the delinquent borrower indistinguishable from a common thief. We must change this opinion by developing a rapport with the lender's team and putting a human face on the borrower; explaining in detail how this mess happened, admit mistakes, and propose workable plans for repayment. When this explanation is coupled with a token gesture or two showing good faith, the lender's attitude can soften.

Plain old deal fatigue sets in as well, which is another reason delaying is almost always to the borrower's advantage. The asset manager's attitude changes because of simple endurance. We know that people can only stay angry for so long, and we are trying to avoid feeding that anger if at all possible. Anger requires energy and needs feeding. If we endeavor to be cooperative instead of contentious, the other side won't have any new reasons to be angry and, hopefully, few reminders of why they're angry in the first place.

Starving the anger by being cooperative is the optimistic scenario. We must always be prepared to respond in kind to a provocation. If the other side wants to throw hammers, we brought a whole crate full of them, and we can play the game that way.

The resolution and settlement of the case typically involves the borrower giving in a little more than we hoped but nevertheless surviving, and the lender's people giving thanks for reaching an agreement that didn't get them fired, closing the file, and moving on to the next case without much thought because the money isn't theirs. A point arrives in the process where we need to stop fighting the lender and do the deal. Think of it as a chart similar to a supply and demand price determiner from Economics 101: the x-axis is how good the deal is for the borrower, and the y-axis is the amount of pain the deal would inflict on the borrower.[16]

When we reach the point where we want to get the deal done and are comfortable that we've moved the lender as far as we can, and the borrower can survive, the time to settle the case has arrived. If the borrower gets greedy

---

[16] For a ridiculous yet incredible over-analysis of this concept, see H. Stanley Jevon, *Essays on Economics (MacMillan & Co., Ltd., 1905), pp. 1-197.*

and tries to continue beyond this point to get a better deal, it will backfire every time. You need to know what is within the lender's realm of possibilities as much as the borrower's.

Chapter 13

Defining "within the realm of the possible."

As we discussed, a settlement 'acceptable to the borrower' doesn't necessarily mean that the borrower satisfying its obligations in the settlement is 'within the realm of the possible.'

No matter how sophisticated, business owners who negotiate with the creditors themselves or through legal counsel won't see the forest for the trees. They are so focused on making the problem go away that they fail to consider whether a settlement is possible to perform.

We hear lawyers boast that their client's lender agreed to take a $2 million settlement on a $4 million loan, but those numbers don't mean anything. That sounds impressive, and I'm sure the borrower is proud of their (or their lawyer's) negotiating skill, but the size of the discount doesn't mean you've made a good deal on the assets. We need more information.

- Is the collateral worth more than $2 million, or do you have cash with which to put in more equity, and does that make economic sense?
- Does the company or project produce income sufficient to service $2 million in debt?
- Are lenders even lending against that type of collateral right now?
- What if the new lender requires that the new loan be amortized on a 15- or 20-year schedule? Can you afford the payments then?
- Can you or someone else personally guarantee the loan if needed? Do you have the wealth to qualify?
- How long can you feed the loan (not that you would, if we have our way) if the economy goes south?
- How much cushion do you have in your numbers?

Taken to the next derivative, let's say the collateral is worth the $2 million. For how much can you, or the lender, sell the collateral? Can the buyer, even if they want to purchase, get financing themselves?

Lenders look at appraisals, which make judgments based on liquid markets in determining market values. The value of the collateral when times were good is irrelevant when there is no demand today. And without demand for the property, how can anyone determine market value?

Furthermore, does that market value depend on ordinary access to credit? If so, then when lenders aren't lending against that collateral, what's the value? You may have figured out that in this example we are asking the same questions about the $2 million discount that are used with a lender to poke at their appraised values. "That's a nice value, but how much is it worth in an illiquid market with no demand, no comparable sales, and no access to credit?"

Absent of other external factors that affect the decision (and make no mistake, there always are), if the answer to any one of these questions is unsatisfactory, settling at $2 million is a bad idea. We would advise to not settle and continue to fight and negotiate, fight and negotiate. As painful as it may be to refuse to make a $2 million deal, by doing so the borrower would be kicking the can down the road at best and sowing the seeds of a worse demise in the future.

April, 2012

The attorney was a well-respected trial lawyer but had only done a few cases involving lenders vs. borrowers. His client had a number of problem loans, and the lawyer had been negotiating with the lenders. On one of the loans, the lender agreed to settle with a partial discount. The original loan was for $1.4 million. The lawyer had negotiated a settlement of $800,000.

Because our client was likely to lose the court case, the attorney thought 57 cents on the dollar was a great deal and, initially, advised the client to accept the settlement offer. Fortunately, during this same time period we were advising the lawyer on strategy in a different case with a similar client and achieved a successful result. Before he accepted the bank's offer on behalf of the client, he decided to let us evaluate this case, give him our opinion on the bank's settlement proposal, and evaluate potential alternative strategies and proposals.

As we came to thoroughly understand the client's entire situation and the lender's condition and goals, we showed him the ways to demonstrate to the lender that the $800,000 settlement was not feasible. After we came in and spent four months in talks with the lender, we were able to negotiate a settlement wherein the lender agreed to accept $375,000 in exchange for a full release of our client.

This was another case of the attorney not seeing the business forest for the legal trees. The attorney had carefully evaluated the strengths and weaknesses of the case and the likely outcome at trial. Reading documents and correspondence with the lender, evaluating the sufficiency of the evidence, and deriving legal theories to defend a borrower are essential duties of legal counsel.

However, many other issues have importance in workout and restructuring negotiations. First and foremost, where is our client coming up with $800,000? Is acquiring that kind of cash even plausible? The lender had rejected alternative proposals, citing regulatory requirements and internal bank policies. Were these reasons legitimate? In our prior experiences with this bank's asset manager on other cases, we knew what types of settlement structures our special assets officer could get approved. Did the bank have an open-and-shut case that would yield them an easy judgment?

In these cases, the borrower usually has limited resources to deploy but may have many good options to defend, delay, or even defeat the bank's lawsuit. But will the cost be worth it, or even necessary? Creative alternatives to court battles always exist if you know where to look, and this requires learning *all* of the facts, especially the financial situation, not only the facts relevant to the legal defense. After you learn all of the facts, the solution may be obvious. But the solution has to satisfy the lender's needs as well as the borrowers. After you determine the best solution comes the hard work of convincing the lender of the same.

> *Accomplishing this doesn't involve persuasion. You will rarely persuade an asset manager to your point of view. Asset managers are not persuaded by much of anything except paying what you owe. Remember, your lender believes you are a scallywag, a reprobate, and a liar to boot. The asset managers will naturally look upon our proposals suspiciously. And they will reject proposals without offering any alternative, which is extremely frustrating for the borrower's side.*

So how do you get it done? We find that the best way to get the lender to accept the best solution is to demonstrate that any more favorable solution for the lender is impossible to accomplish. This means that when you decide on the most favorable outcome for the borrower, at the beginning of the case, you don't propose it.

Initially, you may make proposals nowhere close to what you want. You take the lender's technique (clever, in their mind) of rejecting without countering and use it against them. Make proposal after proposal, and let them give rejection after rejection, and we start crossing off possible outcomes from the list. We cross off the possibilities until only one remains—the one we wanted all along.

From a client management perspective, over time the piles of rejection, though disheartening at the time, makes them feel better because they can tell the story of all of the lender's rejections to others[17]. A pile of rejections also

---

[17] *"In this case [the borrower] wins by demonstrating that the creditor is greedy, ruthless and untrustworthy. The two most obvious advantages of this are (1) it strengthens [the borrower's] existential position, which is a disguised form of "all creditors are grasping," and (2) it offers a large external social gain, since he is now in a position to abuse the creditor openly to his friends without losing his own status as a "Good Joe." He may also*

helps if the case later goes to mediation—the mediator is likely an ex-judge or big-firm lawyer who, if he's ever done a debtor/creditor mediation, represented banks, or if he's done debtor/creditor mediations has only seen debtors who don't make any thoughtful proposals and/or are very contentious.

When receiving any counterproposals, you must be nimble. Quickly assemble all data you need to demonstrate why the offer can't work, and respond without delay, unless the borrower's situation demands delay for as long as possible. The quicker we respond, the more likely the asset manager will review what we send. If we wait three weeks to respond, the asset manager may never look at it because he would have to spend additional time to go back and refresh his memory on the case. Nobody likes doing that, so the asset manager naturally will stick the information in a file and forget about the case until his boss starts asking questions again.

A lender's rejection of an offer is a golden opportunity to communicate the creditor's story to the asset manager. Don't waste the opportunity.

Also remember the best solution will change over time with the circumstances, and the best solution may be a proposal the lender rejected previously. The asset manager will have forgotten about it. We've resubmitted previously rejected proposals many times, knowing the offer was exactly the same, and not once had anyone on the other side notice. Even if they did, the discussion simply becomes another opportunity to tell the story to the lender, explaining why what wouldn't work before is the best option.

---

exploit further internal social gain by confronting the creditor himself. In addition, it vindicates his taking advantage of the credit system [in the first place]: if that is the way creditors are, as he has now shown, why pay anybody." Eric Berne, *Games People Play* (chapter 6, Life Games, "Debtor"), Tantor eBooks. Kindle Edition.

Chapter 14

The Truth (Properly Presented) Shall Set You Free

Successor Bank Loses Big Fish

June, 2009

A CEO of a publicly traded company guaranteed a large acquisition and development loan for a friend who was a developer. Neither the lots nor the homes were selling. The bank failed, and a loss share bank took over. When loan came up for renewal, the new lender would not agree to renew, and they made a demand on our client for payment. His attorney contacted us to see what if anything could be done.

The lender saw dollar signs on our client's forehead because of his income and stock portfolio. The CEO also had most of his assets protected in trusts or otherwise long before he guaranteed this loan, which he had disclosed to the lender when the loan was made.

Asset protection structures drive asset managers out of their minds. However, when the borrower has protected assets, the lender will be particularly aggressive with litigation and particularly difficult in negotiations. They will stand firm and be unreasonable.

An even worse situation is when the borrower has assets the lender could theoretically attach if it obtained a judgment, but we show them the unintended consequences of their demands will lower their amount collected.

The client's company had also received bad publicity of late and the current share price was unusually low. More importantly, the stock wasn't trading very often. Just because a stock trades on an exchange doesn't necessarily mean the stock is liquid. The lender did not think about how, as CEO of a publicly traded company, he could not liquidate millions of dollars in company stock even in the best of circumstances. Securities regulations would require him to disclose the transaction (because he is an insider), which would cause the stock to crater, resulting in his termination. Selling the stock wasn't an option. If the bank obtained a judgment against him, he would also be fired and possibly lose all of his options because of perceived "bad acts."

Furthermore, this successor lender did not do the hard work of reading and understanding their own loan documents. They were only focused on a guarantor with the ability, but not the obligation, to pay off the loan. These weren't the former bank's standard form loan documents, and the personal guarantee turned out to favor our client, making it difficult, time intensive and expensive for them to pursue him as guarantor.

Even though the documentation was vague and likely impossible to enforce, the lender decided to sue. We educated our client's attorney on the documentation, and our primary defense was that the lender was required to exhaust their collection efforts against our client's developer partner (our client provided the equity, the developer was to run the business of creating this subdivision of multimillion dollar homes).

The provision was strangely worded, providing the bank must "exhaust *all* collections efforts" against the borrower and the other guarantor. The lender had not foreclosed on the property, had not obtained a judgment against the developer, and had made no collection efforts whatsoever against him. The developer partner had no assets the bank could get (he had no money), but we argued this didn't matter. Therefore, the lender's action was premature and should be dismissed.

Months into a legal process, while the bank still maintained they had the right to pursue our client under the guarantee, they decided to consider a discounted payoff to reach a settlement. The lender had no desire to foreclose on yet more vacant residential lots, and we persuaded them to allow our client to buy out the developer's interest in the property in exchange for a payment to the lender close enough to the depressed value of the land. The settlement was advantageous to both our client and the lender.

The Necessity of Research Outside the Loan History

July, 2013

A retired couple had heard the stories of many of their friends buying and selling land along Florida's Gulf Coast for staggering profits. Everybody is doing it, so it must be a good idea. They invested a sizable portion of their nest egg into a piece of waterfront property. Their lender had financed many of these projects, and a large regional bank eventually acquired it when land values crashed. The couple did not have the means or desire to pay large sums to the new lender for a short-term extension on a deeply underwater loan.

We carefully reviewed their loan documents and researched the public records. Something smelled fishy about this deal. In the public real estate and tax records, we learned their land had been bought and sold several times in the months prior to their purchase, each time at drastically higher prices. The clients had kept a copy of their appraisal from the loan, and the appraisal failed to properly reference the recent transactions as required by law and best practices.

We realized that without their knowledge, they were victims of a mortgage fraud scheme. We weren't sure who, but somewhere between the original developer, the appraiser, and possibly even the loan officer at the former bank, someone artificially inflated the value of the property. The property was never worth anywhere near what they paid for it. Our guess was the appraiser and developer were in on the scheme and the banker practiced willful blindness—he/she was collecting good commissions on the origination fees for the loans.

We laid out the circumstances to the lender that acquired the loan. We also explained the couple's financial situation, their income, assets, and also provided information to demonstrate the husband was in poor health and had no business enduring the stress of a lawsuit or other high-pressure collection tactics. The couple was the innocent victim of fraud by the developer (who had since disappeared and could not be located), possibly even with the knowledge of people at the former bank. We could never know for sure.

The attorneys to whom we referred this case did a good job of conveying our concerns to the lender's counsel as well. This case did not need to proceed down the usual course of both sides throwing hammers.

Fortunately for everyone involved, the lender agreed to a reasonable settlement of 25 cents on the dollar, which included taking back the property. The couple was glad to be rid of the property. The process of settling a problem loan does not always have to be contentious. The lender shared everyone's concern about the circumstances surrounding the original loan by the former bank, and the borrower's physical health. All parties were glad to settle the whole unfortunate matter.

Understand Every Word of Binding Agreements

Always carefully scrutinize any documents executed by the borrower subsequent to the original closing. Extensions and modifications are usually sloppy documents. The parties are usually up against a deadline, and time pressure causes lack of attention to detail and drafting mistakes.

Compare defined terms. Look for statements contradictory to provisions in the loan documents. Search for defined words in the loan documents not specifically defined or capitalized, such as a defined term in the amending document. Scrutinize the boilerplate language that addresses the interpretation of discrepancies between amending documents and the original loan documents.

The more times the borrower and lender have modified the original agreements, the more likely you will find a mistake to work with.

March, 2012

A real estate investor had never missed a payment on his performing loan with a regional bank. After a few renewals that were documented by one-page renewal agreements, the bank notified the borrower at renewal time that he was going to have to reapply as if the renewal were a brand new loan.

Fortunately for us, he was obsessive-compulsive, overly detail-oriented, a hoarder, and a pack rat who had kept every e-mail, document, and scrap of paper related to the loan. He had two large boxes of documents and letters. As we carefully examined the paperwork, we discovered the bank had used an inducement to get his loan.

The loan officer wanted to raise the interest rate on the loan by more than 2 percent, demand a 20 percent principal reduction, and shorten the amortization period to 15 years rather than the current 20. The loan was secured by income-producing real estate, and the bank's underwriting criteria had changed for the worse. The bank would never originate a loan at that time on the client's old terms.

The process was long and drawn out because the bank tried to use their committee process and in-house counsel to scare our client into agreeing to a modification that would leave him in worse shape than if he did nothing and went into default. And they surely would have if we weren't involved and hadn't read the documents. Based on the documentation, we were able, even after many attempts on the bank's part to change the terms of the loan, to hold their feet to the fire and make them renew his loan on the same terms for another three years.

We met with the bank's attorneys and demonstrated to them how one sentence, in a document that the bank prepared and the parties executed, obligated the bank to renew the loan on the same terms. The first amendment to the loan documents provided that if the borrower performed each and every covenant in the loan, lender shall renew the loan on the same terms. We argued that not only had our client performed, but also showed, via documentation the client retained, that the provision on the renewal was heavily negotiated and an essential inducement for the client to renew the loan—at that time, the bank was desperate to keep him as a customer.

In the end, that he had kept excellent records was the difference. Our client was pleased that he was able to save a great deal of money. The bank didn't get what they initially wanted, but they did avoid litigation and collection expenses and kept what would have been a problem loan performing. The settlement was a win-win.

When the bank pressured the client, his immediate thought was, "I owe the money, I signed a note, and the loan is due, so how do I pay it? Where do I go to borrow more money?" When you first learn of this type of situation, instead ask these questions: "Why is the bank putting pressure on me? Why the big rush? What are my obligations? What do the documents specifically require of me? Has the bank performed all of its obligations?" The answers to these questions will dictate a large part of your negotiating posture, leverage against creditors, potential outcomes, and overall strategy in dealing with the problem.

We suspect, but do not know, that they knew full well what the documents said, and they also thought that this particular borrower, being neurotic and extremely conflict averse, would simply comply without question. As consultants we were under pressure because the client made clear that if the bank did file a lawsuit, he would pay them off in full immediately. At least the client knew himself: he was a great real estate investor but knew he couldn't handle the pressure of litigation.

What if the situation with the borrower is the opposite, and the borrower has little to no documentation at all, or ability to establish the facts about its financial condition?

The bankruptcy court addressed these issues in the case of *Harrington vs. Simmons,*[18] a cautionary tale of a real estate investor who thought he could

---

[18] *Harrington v. Simmons (In re Simmons)*, 513 B.R. 161 (Bankr. D. Mass. 2014). See also Rudolph Massa, Jr. and James Schu, Jr. *Debtors May Be Denied Discharge for Inadequate Financial Records,* The Legal Intelligencer, February 6, 2015. www.DuaneMorris.com/site/listings/articles.html.

say, "I lost all of my money," without having the documentation to back up his claims.

Individual debtors seeking a discharge of their debts must provide a coherent explanation of profit and loss, together with an explanation of the disposition of assets. It will most probably not suffice to complain that they blindly and willingly took the bad advice of a third party. Even the most unsophisticated individual debtors must be able to adequately account for the financial straits in which they find themselves, and they should go to all reasonable lengths to maintain adequate records or be prepared to justifiably explain failing to do so.

Proper documentation in a presentable format is essential for companies in financial distress, but bankruptcy court is not the only reason, or even the most important reason.

A bankruptcy debtor gets almost all of the benefit of the doubt over creditors in bankruptcy court. Preventing discharge is difficult for creditors, but two exceptions exist: (1) where a debtor unjustifiably fails to keep or preserve sufficient records from which his or her financial condition or business transactions might be ascertained, and (2) where a debtor fails to satisfactorily explain his or her loss or deficiency of assets.

While the first exception "does not require flawless recordkeeping," debtors must still produce sufficient records to allow creditors and the court to ascertain the financial picture. Moreover, while the second exception allows a debtor to explain the disposition of assets, the debtor must corroborate the explanation by providing sufficient evidence.

If a borrower can demonstrate to creditors the likely outcome in bankruptcy, with documentation to back up their claim, perhaps the debtor can avoid bankruptcy and reach a favorable settlement. Although, not always.

Proper records can also avoid litigation. Usually. Saving all paper and electronic files can also come in handy to make creditors comply with their own agreements. Almost always.

The importance of fully responding to lender requests for information.

March, 2011

The owner of a professional architecture firm had a line of credit with a large national bank. His firm drew plans for multimillion dollar custom homes. When the housing economy was strong, he would use the line of credit to cover accounts payable and payroll between milestone payments from clients. As the housing market slowed down, he saw more and more situations where he had staff engaged in making plans and servicing projects, only to have the project canceled before completion or having delivery refused.

The abysmal cash flow of the business would not enable him to pay the line of credit. New business wasn't coming in; the payment history was spotty at best; the firm had laid off a number of professionals and support staff and otherwise downsized to remain viable.

The well-respected firm had downsized to only himself. He had become a one-man office, only part-time. He had a second part-time job at a hardware store. He went from a major player in his industry to merely trying to find work to pay his bills. But he still owed the entire balance of the line of credit and had no way to pay back the money.

Thankfully, the lender was interested in settlement discussions in the hope of avoiding litigation. We carefully painted a detailed picture of his financial situation, which required weeks of meetings with the client and his accountants, to demonstrate how his business had dwindled to almost zero.

The discussions with the bank were darkly humorous. It was 2012, the bottom of the housing bust that caused the Financial Crisis. No homes had been built for years, the housing market had come to a halt, and foreclosures were everywhere. Yet, here we were, in a convoluted dialogue with one of the world's biggest banks, having to repeatedly explain how and why business had dried up for a designer of million dollar and higher luxury homes.

Personally he had no liquid assets, so we analyzed what could be collected from his business (accounts receivable, many from bankrupt builders, office furniture, equipment, architectural drafting tools, etc.) and demonstrated that the lender would collect less than it would cost to turn these assets into cash. We also showed how little a wage garnishment of his part-time jobs would realize. After a long process, the lender accepted a lump sum payment of 10 cents on the dollar to satisfy the loan and cancel his personal guarantee. He was able to avoid personal bankruptcy and bankruptcy of his company.

The settlement right-sized his balance sheet such that he could continue his practice on a cash basis going forward to build his business and build his reserves. Through a painstaking process of patiently explaining his story to the bank, we achieved one of our best settlements. The best news of all was that as the case settled, the market for luxury home construction rebounded.

The Importance of Promptly Responding to Creditor Communication

You cannot win them all. With one exception (discussed in the next section), in the cases we handled with bad outcomes, the bad outcome was the result of one of two problems with the case:

1. Our own client's legal counsel, or
2. Our own client's, or his advisors', lack of responsiveness to our requests for information

One of our longest and most bitterly contested cases ended unfavorably because of our client not providing the bank information in a timely manner. After fighting with the bank from pillar to post for over two years, litigation, fights over document production, contempt motions, bankruptcy of the operating entity, and hard feelings all around, we had the bank ready to settle. The lender would accept a discount of 55 cents on the dollar if the borrower dismissed the litigation and bankruptcy cases, and the bank further offered the borrower 12 months to source financing for the payoff.

We eagerly accepted the offer. As discussed previously, the asset manager with whom you are dealing has no real negotiating power. Standard procedure when a deal is struck is for the borrower to provide updated financial statements and several other documents needed to fill the asset managers file, so he can present the settlement to his committee for approval. This takes a few frustrating weeks for everyone.

Our client was a quirky old bird, and this wasn't the first time he "checked out" on us. But it was the last. We could not beg, cajole, persuade, or even threaten him to get his financials updated along with the bank's other document requests. We had to run interference with the bank to keep the settlement viable.

If the client had been responsive, and we had promptly provided financials that showed the situation at that time, the bank wouldn't have asked for any more financial information. But instead, three months passed before we finally delivered everything they needed and waited for our answer.

The answer was terrible. Good news was now bad news. During the 3 months between the date of the original agreement and when we finally pried all of the information from the borrower and sent it to the bank for approval, the client's business had improved, a lease on the property in default was performing again, and he had signed a new major tenant, in spite of us vehemently objecting. The economics of the collateral was different, and the original settlement was too generous.

The bank backed out of the deal. We tried a motion to enforce the settlement agreement, but the bank knew the motion was a loser and threatened an abusive litigation claim against our client and his attorney. His attorney withdrew the motion.

We resigned from the case because we doubted our ability to be effective with the bank anymore. The client's actions destroyed our credibility. The bank didn't believe the property had drastically improved in three months, but it had. The asset manager insinuated that we had fudged the numbers previously to get the settlement.

In the end, the ex-client's case was a total loss for him. He agreed to all of the bank's demands and left his attorneys with huge unpaid legal bills.

Chapter 15

When to Stop Paying

A borrower in a distressed loan situation must carefully consider every use of its available cash. We must consider several options, particularly if the borrower can make the payments and the business or property has cash flow. If the loan reached maturity and the lender wants a large reduction in principal or to increase the interest rate or shorten the amortization, when and how to make payment to the lender on the loan depends upon the unique circumstances and the type of lender. Continuing to make payments until there isn't any cash left will only result in the business failing and the lender taking the collateral because the borrower has no money left for a legal defense.

Ninety-nine percent of the time, if the borrower is making the payments, the lender will not even talk about restructuring a debt. The borrower is paying, is expected to pay, and will continue to pay. That is the lender's attitude.

The process begins, necessarily, with the borrower intentionally defaulting on the loan. Many times this happens in a passive manner: the loan matures, and the borrower doesn't pay off the balance. Or the borrower runs out of money and can't pay even if they wanted to.

Our rule of thumb for "when to stop paying" in other situations:

If the borrower can make the loan payments, they should continue to make the loan payments unless we determine (a) the borrower has no chance of refinancing the loan at maturity, (b) that because of external factors affecting the borrower, a payment default in the future is a certainty, (c) continuing payments on the loan will necessarily cause other financing to default, (d) continuing payments will eventually put the borrower out of business, or (e) the current cash flow of the business is insufficient to cover debt service, and the business does not have cash reserves to cover the shortfall without the guarantor stepping in to cover the shortfall (i.e., "feed the loan").

With few exceptions, when any of these circumstances exist, the borrower should stop paying immediately. We would advise the borrower to immediately stop paying on *all* loans of that borrower entity, except for operating lines of credit that keep the company in business, and loans with a cash collection lockbox feature, obviously (the only remedy there being a bankruptcy filing, unless the loan documents provide otherwise).

Stopping payment when the guarantor (or other owners/investors) must feed the loan to cover debt service depends on the situation. Obviously, in a startup situation, anticipated and unanticipated capital calls happen all of the time. Sometimes the cash flow shortfall was anticipated, or is expected to be a short-term issue from which the business will quickly recover.

But if the business is failing because of operational problems or is subject to an external economic shock, we have to look at the business and determine, to the best of our ability, the likelihood of recovery without defaulting on the debt payments. This is always a tough situation and decision, and we have to work to overcome the client's optimism. Business owners always see sunny days ahead; that's why they are business owners in the first place.

Our job is to inject the reality of the situation into the decision-making process and to persuade the owner that a payment default or bankruptcy reorganization filing—*now*—is best for the business to survive and offers the borrower the best chance of successfully restructuring its debts. The most persuasive argument is always that if the loan requires feeding, defaulting preserves cash that may be used to keep operations going and, more importantly, to pay legal fees.

The Account Sweep—An Important Cautionary Tale

Most loan documents provide that a bank can sweep *all* of the money in any of the borrower's accounts upon a default. No lawsuit necessary. And if the borrower doesn't have the money to bring the loan current, the bank will apply the proceeds first to a bunch of fees you never thought about before, then back interest, then principal.

July 2013

A successful salesman suffered a maturity default on loan for an ill-advised real estate investment purchase, and his wife had her nest egg of around $50,000 in a bank account at Wachovia National Bank. Wachovia failed, and Wells Fargo, who was the lender on the man's shopping center loan, acquired all of Wachovia's assets, including her account.

It didn't occur to either the husband or the wife that when the wife opened the account, they made the account a joint account between the two of them.

The property never cash flowed enough to make the payments. The husband, who personally guaranteed the loan, spent five years covering the shortfall out of his personal cash. After he'd fed the loan for five years, Wells Fargo refused to renew it or extend it. Days after the loan matured, the bank used its power under the loan's "dragnet clause" to sweep the wife's cash out of the account. Money that she earned from her own career—the family emergency fund. Gone.

Unless specifically required by the loan documents, close –or never open– savings, checking, money market, or any other accounts at a financial institution who loans the borrower or guarantors money (or negotiate out any "dragnet clause" in the loan documents before closing).

Defaulting on a loan you can pay to try to "get a deal" is always a bad idea. Situations may occur wherein a borrower may be tempted to quit paying a loan in an attempt to get a deal from the lender. This rarely works without committing fraud, and even when it does work, the effort is rarely worth it, particularly if the loan is in the borrower's personal name. One such case was the only case in which we were involved where ultimately the borrower paid off the loan in full.

February, 2014

The borrower had protected his assets and income as well as possible in his situation. The objective was not to get the biggest discount ever, but our client demanded concessions to settle.

Acrimony was not in short supply. For various reasons, the borrower felt that the bank had misrepresented many facts and was involved in fraudulent acts with the developer of the project, who had filed for bankruptcy. Meanwhile, the lender was not happy that we had put up such a fight—over three years without paying on the loan, the accusations against the bank, and generally outfoxing their lawyers at every turn.

But a fox of a different kind arrived on the scene. Over the course of three years, the lender had obtained a judgment against the client and his wife, who co-signed on the loan. The bank commenced collections efforts with an aggressive collections law firm, but we managed to delay and frustrate the lender's collections efforts.

Other than their personal "stuff," everything they owned was encumbered by loans. Liquid assets were in LLC entities in which the borrower could not control distributions; he was self-employed and could therefore control his personal income and expenses to a great extent. We were ready to play defense until the lender accepted one of our many settlement offers.

One sunny morning in May, everything changed: the husband paid off the loan, in full with interest.

One sunny morning in May, a county sheriff's deputy showed up at the couple's door with a writ of possession and a tow truck. The truck towed away the wife's Cadillac from the driveway and to the auction yard.

The car wouldn't fetch $10,000 if sold. It was 15 years old and had 120,000 miles on it. It'd be a drop in the bucket against the judgment. But the car didn't have a loan against it, and the wife co-signed the loan and was subject to the judgment.

Moreover, the Cadillac was mama's pride and joy. In post-judgment discovery, the bank's attorney must've detected the wife's great attachment to the car, or they were angry and wanted to hit the only spot they could, or maybe it was a lucky guess.

> *"Appear at points which the enemy must hasten to defend; march swiftly to places where you are not expected."*
>
> – Sun Tzu, The Art of War

Checkmate. Game, set, and match. Sometimes you're the windshield, and sometimes you're the bug. This move was brilliant. Regardless of the lender's rationale, the case was over.

The two lessons are: (1) maybe you feel you were misled, or ripped off and don't deserve it, but if you can make the payments, make the payments, and (2) NEVER have a spouse co-sign on a loan or guarantee if they are not active in the business and essential to the financing. We had many wealthy clients after the financial crisis that had bought vacation homes or second home lots in their personal name. The 90 percent decline in real estate values in overbuilt mountain, lake and beach vacation destinations brought down many small business owners in the Great Recession.

The gray area in which this case resided, however, was that the term of the loan still had many years to go, and chances that the real estate collateral would recover enough value to enable the borrower to refinance were near zero. The borrower was looking at losing a small fortune on this project, but he could take the hit. Its failure would not put him into bankruptcy. If we were reasonably certain that the borrower couldn't make the balloon payment without financing, then stopping payments might be a reasonable option. In that situation, when we don't believe the borrower will obtain financing for the takeout, we can explain the situation to the lender, and try—or at least appear—to be cooperative.

Stopping payment might make sense if the borrower could produce evidence of fraud or misrepresentation or other lender liability claims. The evidence wouldn't need to be ironclad proof, a smoking gun, but the evidence should be enough that if a few assumptions turn out to be true, the borrower might get past the bank's summary judgment. If we can put a small measure of doubt into the bank's mind about the merits of the claims (or more accurately, about a judge's opinion as to the merits of the claims), the bank has a strong incentive to settle.

Otherwise, the best course is taking the medicine of a bad deal and moving on.

The case wasn't a total loss, however. Over the course of three years, the value of the property had increased, at least according to the bank's appraisal. Although the property was still worth less than the loan balance, the lender was able to give the borrower more credit for the property at foreclosure. Also the borrower had the benefit of not making payments over all of that time, but a portion of that savings went for legal fees.

Importantly, the borrower was also able to obtain financing of the payoff to the lender, which was not possible three years earlier. Because of the judgment, the borrower could not get a bank loan, so he borrowed money from a retirement account to pay off the bank. When the bank canceled the judgment, he borrowed money from a bank to put back into the retirement account in time to avoid penalties for early withdrawal.

In the end, the borrower ended up better off than if he paid the loan until maturity and accepted the bank's offers of one-year extensions and large principal pay downs. But the outcome was nowhere near the cost and almost led to a divorce!

Chapter 16

Castling the King

Castling the king is an unusual defensive chess tactic and the only way that enables a player to move two pieces at once. Basically, if both are unmoved in the match, the king and either rook change places. This particular move is a defensive strategy that accomplishes two goals. First, the king is in better defensive corner position, well protected by pawns and a rook. Second, the rook is closer to the center, where he is more maneuverable and can provide a better defense.

Targeted Strategic Default in Multiple Loan Situations

April, 2009

A residential builder and developer had almost $18 million in contingent liabilities (personal guarantees of his business loans). The collateral was primarily residential lots, homes under construction, spec homes, and land. He had two loans on one project and he was making all of his payments on time. When his bank failed, the acquiring bank put him between a rock and a hard place. The new lender gave him six months to refinance, or they would sell his loan.

This particular situation was more common in the early days after the Financial Crisis, when banks and FDIC receivers would use the threat of sale to "vulture investors" as leverage to have the borrower find other financing or give back the property (assuming the lender wanted the property, which varies from case to case).

The guarantor had the resources to make payments, but he was not in a position to pay off the loan, and he could not get a loan at another bank because of tightened credit, especially for anything related to residential lots or construction. If he were to pay off these loans, he would default on all his other loans. He could not pay off this loan because he needed cash to keep making payments on other projects with solid long-term upside.

Here is an instance where strategic default made sense. He had loans on projects that went down the tubes, and he had good projects, but his problem is he had personally guaranteed both the good and the bad. Not being able to pay off the loans on the bad projects could cause him to lose the good projects as well.

But this lender didn't care about that at all. Their objective was to collect everything possible on their loans, even if it causes other defaults. The bank has an incentive to be aggressive before the other loans default. The borrower's argument was that using all available cash would drive him into bankruptcy, and the bank might have a preference issue with the payoff if made within 90 days of filing for bankruptcy.

After months of negotiation the key issue was the contingent liabilities. The lender would not approve a discounted payoff of the loan that would allow the borrower to keep the property; they were concerned that if anything happened to the borrower after the settlement, a bankruptcy court might unwind the transaction and make the bank pay the proceeds back to the court.

If the borrower "did the right thing" and refinanced with a new lender on expensive terms, which would ultimately drive him to bankruptcy, the other creditors could have claims against the bank under murky, complicated 'deepening insolvency' causes of action beyond the scope of this work.

Fortunately, the macroeconomic climate made the decision even more complicated for the lender, which we were more than happy to emphasize.

This particular loan resolution required approval by the FDIC, and the regulators were looking at the local community banking environment carefully. Most of the other loans were large loans with other small community banks, and a bankruptcy filing affecting the other $18 million in loans would move another vulnerable bank closer to failing. The lender agreed to, and the FDIC approved, a settlement of a discounted payoff at 45 cents on the dollar.

The borrower kept the property because the bank was persuaded that, in their hands, the collateral was illiquid, and the cost of litigation, foreclosure, maintenance, and sale would exceed any amount collected from the sale.

After agreeing to this settlement, the lender mysteriously backed out of their agreement. Understandably, the borrower was upset. Rather than filing suit to enforce the settlement, we instead decided to wait for their next move. Three months later, the bank notified us that they changed their mind and would take the settlement.

Unfortunately for the bank, the local economy was in even worse shape than before, property values continued their decline, and the client's source of funds cut their loan amount by $50,000.[19] Faced with the options of accepting the lower amount or heading into litigation over the loan default, and our counterclaims to enforce the settlement, the bank accepted the reduced offer. The bank may have been trying to exert pressure on the borrower, but the delay cost the bank an additional $50,000.

---

[19] In other words, we re-traded the bank. Really, how could we not? When a party does not respond to an offer for an unusually long amount of time then suddenly accepts, they have a reason. Almost always, that reason is that party's situation has changed for the worse. Taking advantage of the situation depends on the relationship. No possibility existed for any continuing relationship among the parties. They were also jerks. We didn't feel the least bit bad about re-trading the deal.

This case provides useful insight into how regulators sometimes help, and the following case provides useful insight into bank disconnect from reality.

Strategic Default Due to Decline in Collateral Value

September, 2010

The owner of an operating business had significant contingent liabilities in a wide variety of real estate projects. One particular project, a speculative purchase of a large tract of raw land for future commercial development, could potentially sink the entire enterprise. Our client's bank failed, and the acquiring bank purchased the loans in a loss-share agreement with the FDIC. The bank wanted a massive principal payment of approximately 40 percent of the loan balance in exchange for a 12-month extension. To make matters worse, the bank demanded a higher interest rate. This was untenable.

Because the land could not produce any positive cash flow, the partners had to fund loan payments out of pocket from other enterprises or from personal funds. Of several original partners in the entity used to purchase the land and borrow the funds, only the client and one other partner made the payments to keep the loan current. The remaining partners had dropped out or been diluted.

The client's primary business was still profitable, but profits were considerably lower. He was trying to keep all of his obligations performing, and he had a net consumption of cash because he was covering all of the taxes, interest, debt service maintenance, etc. Our client had not missed any payments, but he could not manage the 40 percent that the bank demanded.

The asset manager demanded that our client "right–size" the loan because it would not appraise for the loan value. They wanted the balance reduced to 70 percent of their appraised value, which itself was probably double the actual value. If forced to make a large principal payment, he would not have the ability to make the following monthly payments for long. The bank's offer was unacceptable.

This case is an example of the lender's actions making no sense in the context of the case. You will have a more difficult time if your asset manager is a fool instead of one who merely follows orders. All of the same rules apply to the lender's attorney. Perhaps the asset manager hadn't reviewed or didn't understand the documentation. Sometimes the asset manager was taking action on orders from superiors who lack any context at all. Discerning the asset manager's motivation is difficult, but you must quickly determine what type of person the asset manager is.

Unfortunately, in these processes, we not only work with facts, but with personalities and prejudice. Jealousy and irrational assumptions can come into play. The lender's approach to "negotiating" the troubled loan was that because our client "had a lot of money," a nice house and drove a nice car, he should be able to pay.

A trust owned the residence in which he lived, and the trust did not guarantee the loan. He bought the car years ago, long before the loan was ever originated, when his company was extremely profitable. We informed the asset manager that it did not matter where he lived or what he drove. The asset manager's position was that our client must liquidate all of his assets to pay the note.

Often when the lender does act, the action makes no sense whatsoever in the context of the case. Someone higher up the chain of command demanded it, but that person doesn't understand all of the facts of the case. Filing a lawsuit is the most common of these. Usually the bank filing suit against our client is a head scratcher.

The asset manager can also be playing a game of his own. The loan had not matured but would a few months later. Therefore, the loan wasn't in default. We believed the lender stalled the negotiations past the maturity date and then filed the lawsuit they were threatening.

Although litigation was underway, the delays had given us time to thoroughly research every entity owned by the client and the values of all of the assets. The client's financial advisors had taken an approach similar to the lender and relied on appraised values. Nobody dug deep into the facts to have the knowledge of the assets in their marketplace now and going forward. No one had thought about liquidity—if put up for sale today at any price, did buyers even exist?

From a series of meetings over several months in which we educated the lender, the bank agreed to a restructuring of the loan, giving the client terms he needed to turn things around, and dismissed the lawsuit.

We reviewed the assets; how much the creditors, both secured and unsecured, were owed; cash on hand; cash flow; and any value available. We not only understood the borrower's income, assets and capacity to pay, but also which assets were secured in other loans and by whom, the outlook for those loans, the contingent liabilities and the likelihood of default on those loan guarantees, and the outcomes in bankruptcy for each entity and the guarantor of the subject loan.

We analyzed whether each asset was in an entity that could be bankrupted with a viable reorganization plan. We made a chart of all of the assets and showed what entity owned the asset and whether that entity had any obligation under their loan. If no obligation existed, we outlined the governing policies of the operating agreements to establish that what the asset manager demanded wasn't permitted even if the borrower wanted to fund payments from the trust.

The bank's lawsuit worked to our advantage because our client wasn't intimidated by it. The client understood that the case was about facts and math, not the bankers bellyaching about stuff the borrower didn't have to sell. The client's attitude was, "I'll pay the lawyer a big retainer and check in with him about a year from now to hear what we settled for." He had money to fund the legal battle, which is job number one: keeping a reserve of cash safely tucked away to pay lawyers. This is the last line of defense.

How much money should be in this strategic reserve? The amount is dependent on the person's overall liabilities. When the debts run into the millions, the reserve should be at least six figures. Litigating cases of this size can quickly run up legal fees over $50,000, and a complex bankruptcy reorganization can quickly reach six figures. Base this number on the number of loans and entities.

As noted elsewhere, the first thing a borrower should accept is that if they have any cash money or other liquid assets (stocks, bonds, CDs, etc.), they had best be prepared to hand it over to the creditors, their lawyer, or both.

Unless they can get rid of these assets without a fraudulent conveyance, they will have to play "hide and seek" with the cash.

In a very clever move, a gentleman was in trouble on a loan but had $40,000 in his bank account, which of course he didn't want the bank to take. He hired an attorney to deal with the bank's lawyer and gave the lawyer his $40,000 as a retainer.

Now, if the lender had thought to demand the money from the lawyer, the lawyer would turn it over. But we figured this wouldn't occur to the bank because it hadn't occurred to any of us after over 100 workouts. Crafty. You can achieve remarkable results with a bit of imagination, together with a creditor's lack of attention to detail. A professional debt collector would not miss that.

The formerly rich and/or famous borrower.

Another difficult case is when the borrower is a famous person who is no longer wealthy. Stories are everywhere about athletes blowing all of their money on useless junk and lousy investments. One professional athlete, a true crowd favorite in his team's city, had several bad real estate loans from a bank that failed. A new bank acquired his loans in a loss-share transaction with the FDIC.

The athlete had retired but still made a bit of income from broadcasting, personal appearances, speeches, etc. The bank, of course, smelled blood. The borrower had made tens of millions over his career. The contracts weren't a secret; they were on the front page of the sports section. However, the borrower had made several bad real estate investments other than the defaulted loans this bank held.

When he was riding high at the top of his career, this athlete made a terrible mistake. In his divorce he gave up most of his cash to keep his business investments, and the businesses failed. Even his home mortgage was severely underwater. Most people in his predicament would be toast—what assets he had were all worth less than their debt, and his income couldn't cover all of the loan payments, let alone pay off the balances.

Fortunately for this borrower, he was able to keep the creditors working with him by the force of his personality. Also, the bank knew that a lawsuit against him would be a public relations disaster. Because our client built a huge amount of good will in the community from being a great guy and was also a tough as nails competitor who showed no fear, everybody kept calm and worked out reasonable settlement terms.

Another pro athlete, now coaching in the NFL, woke up to find that a creditor had taken his life savings. He had way overpaid for a piece of vacation property at the peak of the market, which was now worth about 15 percent of the loan balance. The lender had obtained a default judgment against him because they had filed a lawsuit to which he did not respond. He was not aware of the lawsuit at all until he received notice that the lender used the judgment to garnish his bank accounts.

Fortunately, we investigated the matter, and his attorney demonstrated to the bank's attorney that the bank served the lawsuit on the wrong man. The borrower could prove he wasn't even in the same state as the property when the sheriff served the lawsuit, and the lawyer found the sheriff deputy who served the papers. The description of the man he served did not match the borrower and certainly was not the description of a pro football player.

The bank's lawyer agreed to void the service and return the money, and the parties later made a reasonable settlement.

Here again—asset protection. The borrower had all of his cash money in one account. Cash money should be spread out among multiple banks, credit unions, or other financial institutions that vary in size and geographic location. A borrower evading a judgment creditor has many other options for protecting cash, but this is always good sense. When the creditor obtains a judgment, the borrower must disclose its assets and the locations. And although the lender still must go through the garnishment procedures in the jurisdiction of the institution (giving the borrower a chance to close the account and move the cash), a sharp collections firm will hunt down the cash eventually.

Again, when the borrower has significant liquidity, you shouldn't let the process go this far. Use other negotiation points to settle with the creditors before they obtain a judgment.

Chapter 17

The Biggest Mistake

The biggest mistake made by borrowers in financial trouble is made every day and almost every time:

> *When creditors will not extend or*
> *restructure existing debts, refinancing*
> *with a new lender is a serious mistake.*

Because?

> *Solving debt problems with additional debt, likely*
> *more expensive debt, eventually leads to disaster.*

Should a Borrower Raise Capital to Pay Off Debt?

For companies and family businesses in distress, financial restructuring depends on effective negotiation with existing creditors, avoiding litigation or bankruptcy where possible, and NOT avoiding litigation where necessary or bankruptcy where advantageous. Each decision along the way depends upon the borrower's financial situation, the business plan, the collateral, the financial strength of the principals, and the cash flow of the assets or lack thereof.

Moreover, feedback from investor contacts can be effective in settlement negotiations with existing creditors. The objective is to achieve a settlement with existing creditors for an amount that can be financed on reasonable terms, working at today's values. Sounds easy enough, yes? In reality this almost never happens because the lender (a) always thinks the borrower is stealing from them, and (b) doesn't change its collection strategy and tactics to conform to financial reality.

First ask yourself why. Does raising money with the existing debt in place solve the problem or merely delay the day of reckoning? Rescue capital is expensive capital. If a company or a project has too much debt, investors are unlikely to commit funds no matter how rosy the upside projections.

A better goal is settling your existing debt first. This allows the borrower to stay in the project at a better ownership level. Accomplishing this is far easier said than done. However, we want to constantly seek interest from third-party investors, lenders, or purchasers as the case may be. The feedback from these sources is useful in renegotiating the debt with your existing lender, primarily from the standpoint of building an evidentiary arsenal to blow holes through the lender's appraisal of the collateral or the financial strength of the guarantor. Feedback from these third parties, particularly when in the form of a written purchase offer or financing term sheet, demonstrates further to the lender why our settlement plan, whatever it may be, is a better recovery for them than foreclosures, lawsuits, etc.

Restructuring a distressed business is fact-dependent upon the assets. It depends on your particular circumstance, what the asset is, the size of the debt, and the cash flow situation. Discuss the situation with lender contacts to determine what sort of financing might be available for the business, property or asset, and use the lender's feedback as a basis for settlement negotiations.

Ironically, many borrowers can obtain new financing from other lenders shortly after settling problem debts. The way to ensure that the borrower will be qualified to borrow money in the future is to successfully achieve settlements with the borrower's current creditors that offer protection going forward. Lenders *have* to loan money to make a profit, and while the lender with whom you settle might not lend to that particular borrower again, they will be able to borrow in future years from other sources as their financial position improves. Doing whatever is necessary to avoid personal bankruptcy is the key to quickly becoming creditworthy.

Staying in the Deal for Potential Upside

December, 2010

A real estate developer owed $20 million on a large tract of strategically situated land. He made large principal reductions for 12-month renewals and had never missed a payment. The lender, a large national bank, had even pressured him into borrowing money against other property he owned to make a $6 million pay down.

The man had been doing real estate deals for several decades and had valuable assets. However, he did not have a large amount of cash or any assets that were unencumbered by loans. To make matters worse, when the bank filed a lawsuit against the client, his attorney admitted that he owed the money and didn't offer a defense. The bank easily obtained summary judgment against the client personally.

> *Sometimes a judgment is not all bad and is another step in the process. Most people think that, like on television, if you get a judgment against someone, and they have money, they have to send you the money. In reality, a judgment is nothing more than a license to attempt to collect.*

The bank's collection efforts went nowhere because his corporate structure was Byzantine by design, as expected from real estate developers (or wealthy people in general). Recovering cash from an interest in an LLC or corporation is difficult, time consuming and expensive. The case boiled down to what the lender would take to allow the borrower to keep the property.

We negotiated aggressively because we knew this property was worth a fraction of the loan amount. We argued and argued and brought them offer after offer in the $2.5-3.0 million range, but the asset manager rejected everything. Our client believed that the property was worth $5 million, but only if he owned it.

This was no greenhorn developer; he was experienced and respected, even by the asset manager. He had the knowledge and experience to put the right product on the land. He had the political muscle to get his zoning case approved with minimal modifications. If he could get himself out of this situation with this lender, he could get financing and receive interest from many potential equity partners.

The asset manager had not disclosed their appraisal (again, the client's lawyer offered no defense), and because the lawsuit had become a judgment they were under no obligation to disclose their appraisal's contents. But watching nonverbal cues during meetings and dissecting carefully worded statements, we thought $4 million was the number and made that offer. And the asset manager rejected it.

Well, we weren't so clever after all. But something remarkable happened. Later that same day, the bank's attorney called and told us that the bank would take $5 million in exchange for a full release of the borrower. We could structure the transaction however we wanted, but it must involve the bank receiving $5 million, and the borrower can't keep the property.

Well, shoot. That won't do. The bank, however, has a problem. If the borrower keeps the property, or any interest in the property, or an ownership interest in an entity that purchases it, then other creditors can attempt to unwind the transaction if our borrower later files for bankruptcy. This would include oral agreements, if proven, to exchange ownership interests in entities that own the property.

Our client insisted that he wouldn't agree to anything unless he could keep the property, and we needed to convince him otherwise. We had a few factors in our favor. First, he wasn't going to be doing any business at all while this bank had a judgment against him personally. Second, he was in poor health from all the stress of the financial problems. If he were to die while the judgment was in place, the bank could soak up any cash the man had after all of the other secured creditors were paid, leaving the heirs, who are, of course, used to living the high life with little to nothing. He needed the judgment to go away.

Third, we had located an investment fund and structured a transaction that would fund the settlement payment to the bank, and they wanted him to stay in the deal. This fund was investors, not operators of real estate, and they understood, as we did, that the value in the property was in the man who owned it. No investor in these situations is going to allow the borrower to stay in the deal with an equity position higher than a nominal amount (which frustrates the clients exceedingly—they always think they deserve more equity, even though they aren't putting any money into the new deal). He would have a way to earn his way back into an ownership interest in the property, and this was key.

The bank wasn't concerned about what happened after the transaction closed. The borrower could get the property back later, even a day later, so long as the borrower can truthfully state that he has no interest in the property or the purchasing entity at the time of closing.

We had to negotiate on the issue of the client's potential repurchase of an interest in the property, and the bank agreed to narrow their overbroad language on the topic in the settlement agreement. Although this did leave open the remote possibility of a fraudulent transfer or preference claim in bankruptcy, we persuaded the bank that this was the best possible outcome for them. [20]

Our client retained a position in the property, escaped the judgment and the liability, and received funding to maintain the property going forward until sales or development. This gave him an upside with no requirement to put additional cash into the deal.

Removing Personal Liability

September, 2010

An operating company with nearly 40 different shareholders: individuals, LLCs, trusts and other entities, defaulted on its $4.5 million line of credit. The originating bank failed, and a new bank purchased the company's loan in a loss-share transaction with the FDIC.

Several successful men, directors of the company, guaranteed the loan. Over time these board members and other investors had poured almost $15 million of capital into the company to fund operations as well as the debt they borrowed and guaranteed. When the loan matured, the board was unsuccessful in negotiating a renewal agreement.

---

[20] In this situation, if the judgment went away, any possibility of the client filing for bankruptcy went with it. We had already settled his other problem loans.

One of the directors personally guaranteeing the loan had a strong net worth as a retired, senior-level executive of a publicly traded company. Fortunately for him, his largest asset was his pension. The creditors would have a difficult time collecting if they went after the pension.

Another one of the guarantors was a real estate developer who had significant contingent liabilities and was using up his liquidity in other struggling entities. The last guarantor was a gentleman with significant assets, many of which were in protected entities—trusts and family limited partnerships—that were not a party to the loan or the guarantee.

They were stuck between a rock and a hard place. Although the company had made sales, it had not yet reached profitability. A critically important contract with a large company fell through because our company was not yet financially stable, and the bank would not renew without that contract in place.

As discussed elsewhere, the "loss-share bank" concept was a disastrous idea come to fruition whose only goal is to collect, not develop a "banking relationship" with the borrowers of the failed bank. The only issues to discuss were the guarantor's ability to pay, and the value of the collateral, which was negligible. The bank had all the equipment, inventory, prototypes and demonstration models as collateral, but they were of limited value, not production models. As usual, the collateral had considerable value if the company was an ongoing business but little value on the auction block for liquidation, especially custom equipment in a bad economy.

While we assisted the asset manager with its understanding of the value of the assets, we also helped our client locate a multibillion dollar investment fund that felt our client had a viable product. They were willing to commit up to $25 million to the company, with specific conditions.

First, they were willing to put only a limited amount of money into retiring the company's debts and obligations. After consulting with us, the investment fund set a target of $1.5 million as the target payoff for the $5 million loan. Next, the fund agreed to invest $8 million if we were able to successfully get all of the company's creditors to agree to accept a discounted amount. The fund also agreed that as the company met certain tiers of benchmarks, they would provide additional capital.

We convinced the asset manager through a painstaking process that foreclosing and/or pursuing the guarantors was a losing proposition. Two of the guarantors had assets from which the bank would have an extremely difficult time collecting, and the other had no assets from which to collect. Also, the likelihood of finding a new equity source to pay off the debt was minimal.

Time was on our side for a change. The fund's offer had an expiration date (a few weeks—we easily persuaded them that a short fuse would enable us to get a better deal with the bank). The bank had two choices—take $1.5 million or get far less in bankruptcy court. There was no time left to source other investors. We will either close on this deal or file for bankruptcy. Period.

Ultimately, the bank agreed to settle the $4.6 million for $1.5 million. The investor's proceeds also paid off other creditors and vendors at a discount (by giving them the same choice as the bank) except for creditors whose debt related to needed ongoing strategic relationship, which were paid in full. The company could continue operations and move forward with a right sized balance sheet, and the guarantors, though significantly diluted, still had their ownership interest and positions on the board of directors of the company.

The lender was not concerned about the guarantors keeping an ownership interest in the property because after the transaction closed, the company had no other creditors remaining. Therefore, nobody would have standing to contest the transaction because there were no other debts.

Chapter 18

When to Take a "Bad" Deal

Evaluating the Merits of a Less-Than-Optimal Settlement Offer

The creditors can garnish wages, which in the abstract is terrifying for the borrower. In reality, the amount the creditor can garnish is relatively small (though any amount is bad). First, the lender can't garnish wages until it gets a judgment, which as we know takes time and money. Second, while state laws vary, generally the percentage of the garnishment runs at 15 to 20 percent of take home pay. The garnishment does not affect money contributed to 401ks[21] or amounts withheld for taxes, Medicare, et al. Although 20 percent is painful, the borrower should be able to survive.

In our cases wage garnishments have been rare. The threat of garnishment changes the strategy we will employ and our expectations of how "success" might look in the case. Clients are rarely if ever aware that laws

---

[21] However, that a lender may challenge unusually large contributions to tax-deferred retirement accounts as a preference or fraudulent transfer, and the bankruptcy court can order these contributions reversed.

prohibit an employer from firing an employee solely because of a garnishment, which amplifies the threat to unknowing borrowers.

Another key consideration when evaluating the case is the nature of the client's job. If the job involves fiduciary responsibilities or state licensing requirements, a judgment may cost the client his career.

April, 2011

A successful salesman decided that it was time to build that second home that he and his wife had always wanted. They purchased an expensive piece of land in an exclusive development in the mountains of West Virginia. They were glad to get into the resort as one of the first owners because values kept rising; the land had turned out to be a good investment.

The stock market crashed, the developer went bankrupt, and the land's value spiraled to 10 percent of their outstanding loan balance. The lender demanded a large cash payment in exchange for a short-term renewal.

Not only was the "appraised value" of the land a fraction of what they paid, the reality of the situation was that there were no buyers at *any* price. An investment group had bought the resort out of bankruptcy and had made plans to rejuvenate the project, but that would be many years from now. The lender, who had funded many land purchases in the area, had no desire to foreclose on the property and instead filed a lawsuit against the salesman and his wife.

Borrowers should always avoid borrowing money in their personal name and should never, ever have a spouse co-sign on a loan, particularly a business loan or discretionary assets such as second homes, investment properties, etc.

The lender proceeded aggressively in the litigation, but we were able to persuade them to agree to mediation. The salesman did not have the ability to pay off the loan but did have good income and an ability to make payments over time. Fortunately for the client, the lender had an appraisal for the property that was, in our opinion, entirely too high and unrealistic. The bank would give them more credit for the property than anyone thought it was worth. A consensual foreclosure made sense.

The salesman also had another problem in that he was an employee of a company. The lender could, if it won a judgment in court, garnish his wages. This would also affect his ability to obtain and keep certain licenses the state required for his line of work. This gave us one advantage in that we could explain to the lender how their collection efforts would cause their potential source of repayment, his commission income, to go away. We negotiated a settlement with the bank that yielded the bank 55 cents on the dollar, with our client making monthly payments over a five-year period.

W-2 employees are particularly vulnerable when borrowing in their own names or guaranteeing loans.

Despite a good case that, in our experience, should be settled for a nominal payment, it made sense to pay the lender more to get the case settled. We tell our clients that any case can be settled quickly if they are willing and able to pay more money to the lender. It made sense. The salesman could get back to work, was rid of his bad investment, and still saved a good bit of money. The lender ended up taking a loss but recovered more in less time than they would have by aggressively pursuing collection on a judgment, which would've cost the salesman his job and made the lender's collection efforts fruitless.

The Lender's Financial Condition May Limit Options

July, 2013

An investor owned an entity that bought a number of second home lots. Despite the housing crash, the properties were in good locations, but values would not return to normal for 2 or 3 more years. To our client's disappointment and fear, the lender cut off his line of credit.

He could continue to earn a living and the bank could be paid consistently, but he depended on the line of credit to make the payments on this property when cash flow was tight. He wanted a discounted payoff of the loan but to keep his line of credit. As we evaluated the situation, we knew that a different strategy was going to limit his loss and his exposure.

When we understood how the client operated his business and had structured his personal finances, we all agreed that this lender was not complying with the terms of their own loan documents and had created circumstances that prevented him from paying back his loan. This meant we had lender liability counterclaims we could assert if the bank filed a lawsuit, or, if we wanted to take the initiative, sue the bank first on these causes of action.

In reviewing the loan history and correspondence, we also realized that the lender did not understand that by following its ordinary procedures, they would not only get paid less than the loan balance but might not get anything except yet more undeveloped residential property. We set about educating the lender on the totality of the situation, the unique structure of this company and the guarantor, the current marketplace, and issues with the bank's valuation of the company's assets.

Another piece of the puzzle was our client's goals. He had a great deal of cash invested in these assets, and he didn't want to lose them to foreclosure. After evaluating the client's current situation, the outcomes in lawsuits and bankruptcy, and other opportunities in which the company could engage if the case was settled, we decided that giving the properties to the lender made more sense in the long run.

Furthermore, because his particular lender was having financial difficulties, we knew it would take many years to achieve the client's original objective to keep the assets and settle with a discounted payoff. He had a great case, but does it make sense to drag this out? What is the opportunity cost of going the distance for the "best deal" on paper?

The process was lengthy, but despite the bank aggressively going after him personally in court on his personal guarantee, they eventually agreed to a settlement wherein our client gave the bank the property and made a small cash payment, and the lender forgave the remaining deficiency. It made more sense to give the bank the property instead of more cash. The client was satisfied with the outcome because we had helped him understand how resolution of the problem loan fit into his overall financial goals.

Sometimes You Need to Take the Deal

Summer, 2012

Two cases, one client, different outcomes. In the first, we were negotiating with a special servicer on an apartment building upon which the client owed $8 million. We negotiated an agreement wherein the lender would cancel a scheduled foreclosure in exchange for a discounted payoff of $6.8 million. This was not the greatest deal in history, but our client, a large real estate company, could have taken the offer. But they decided against it and gave the property back to the lender. This was a mistake.

The bank foreclosed, and the company and their investors lost all of their investment in the project. There the story could have ended, but it was worse. A competitor stepped in and bought the project for about the same price for which the servicer would have settled with our client. A few months later, the competitor sold the apartment complex for nearly $9 million. The deal was a home run, but not for us.

Focus on the big picture and upside, not the raw numbers of the settlement.

Lesson learned, a year or so later the same client was in default on a $2.5 million loan secured by multiple properties in various states. These were special-purpose facilities needing a specific type of buyer. The properties had value, but the lender would not renew the loans and was threatening foreclosure. The asset manager did offer, as a gesture of good faith and to avoid time and expense, to settle the loans for 90 cents on the dollar. This time our client took our advice and accepted.

To fund the settlement, the company's investors had to provide additional capital, and the client sold one of the properties at a loss. However, the company sold the other properties at prices that enabled them to return the investors' money with a solid return, and the company also made a profit on the transactions.

Did our client pull a fast one on the asset manager? All things considered, the bank obtained the best recovery under the circumstances. Had they foreclosed and marketed the properties as "bank-owned," potential buyers would have offered an even lower price (even though the bank's appraisal showed the properties were worth about the loan balance— assuming an arms-length transaction after an extended marketing period). And the bank would have expenses related to readying the properties for sale, a large real estate commission to pay, and legal expenses related to the foreclosure.

The company sold the properties for more than the bank's appraisal because of their superior knowledge of the marketplace and their real estate experience. They repositioned the remaining properties and effectively marketed them. It's highly unlikely that anyone other than the borrower would have the experience and knowledge of the unique circumstances; most certainly not a huge bank with countless foreclosed properties that need rapid liquidation.

Another factor was at work. The company also had multiple real estate loans in which they reached a settlement with the same lender. In our experience, when a bank settles one defaulted loan with a borrower, they want to terminate the entire relationship with that borrower.

This makes sense in that nobody wants to do business with someone who did not (or could not) honor their agreements. But this position sometimes costs the lender more in the long run. Wanting to terminate its entire relationship with our client was a factor that cost the lender but not the biggest factor.

When Expecting a Big Payday, Settle Before Payday Arrives

January, 2011

An operating business had a $2.8 million loan that matured with a large national bank. The Great Recession was historic in its impact on his company's industry. When he could not work out a renewal or extension with his lender, the client engaged us to help him negotiate.

The owner, who guaranteed the loan to the company, had significant contingent liabilities. His cash holdings had deteriorated severely as he made loan payments to "feed" the debt service on under-performing real estate projects, and he had capital calls to make for other companies in which he was invested.

Another concern with this business was something unusual, a contingent asset. The client had won a lawsuit against a competitor in tort and had a large money judgment and an equity claim on valuable assets. However, the defendant appealed the verdict. Even though those involved in the case were confident that the court would affirm the judgment, nothing is ever certain with court decisions. The judgment was an asset, but its value and date of delivery were unknown.

With the judgment amount in excess of the amount owed to the lender, but under appeal, the lender had little interest. Nobody knows how long the appeal process will take, and if the court of appeals affirmed, the defendant could make further appeal to the Supreme Court. Years could pass before the case would be resolved. We even attempted to borrow money against the judgment without success.

When Expecting a Big Payday, Settle Before Payday Arrives.

We needed to settle his case before the court decided the appeal. The ambiguity of the outcome and the length of the appeal process created doubt with potential lenders and buyers. The judgment was, in essence, a "contingent asset" with an indefinable value. His current bank assigned no value to it.

Another complicating factor was that the value of the assets of the company was far greater than the value of the company as a going concern. However, this was only true because of the company's relationships and experience in the industry. The lender, would liquidate the company assets to the highest bidder, and one of the company's competitors would get a steal of a deal. Because of the time pressure on the judgment and our client's ability to liquidate the assets at significantly higher prices than the bank, it made sense to settle with the lender at a higher number than we could get in an ordinary workout. After several weeks of negotiations, the bank agreed to take 67 cents on the dollar.

With the same facts save for the possibility of a major cash payment from the judgment, we would have delayed the process to give the company a chance to return to profitability while demonstrating to the lender how little they would recover if they chose to liquidate the company themselves. The distressed borrower must carefully consider every use of remaining liquidity. Parting with precious cash to maintain control over the judgment made sense.

Part 4

"Courage is being scared to death... and saddling up anyway."

–John Wayne

Chapter 19

"Great News! You've been sued!"

The main goal is always to settle the case on favorable terms without the need to hire a lawyer. For business owners in financial distress, lawsuits can be beneficial because the outcome is largely irrelevant. A lawsuit by your lender or business partner is only part of the overall problem. The likelihood of a negative outcome will only change your options, not limit them.

The vast majority of people have no idea what "winning" a lawsuit really means.

Consultants Working with Attorneys

When a lender files a lawsuit, the borrower must hire legal counsel in order for any other non-lawyer advisors to negotiate a settlement with that lender. Some courts have held that a non-lawyer advisor negotiating and settling a debt on behalf of a borrower after the creditor has filed a lawsuit is engaged in the Unauthorized Practice of Law.[22]

Attorney-client Privilege: Non-attorney advisors must be mindful of communication, internally and externally, at all times. When you are in litigation, the adverse party's attorney could theoretically make discovery requests of the advisor's correspondence with the client. In reality, this has only occurred in an extremely small number of cases. Consult legal counsel in your state regarding the workings of attorney-client privilege and attorney work-product protections to learn how communication between clients and advisors can often be brought under such privileges.

However, if the creditor obtains a judgment against the client, the creditor may then compel the borrower, now a "judgment debtor," to produce current financial information in a process known as "post-judgment discovery." If you've done your job, the borrower has already provided this information on many prior occasions in conjunction with settlement offers. Disclosing financial information makes it easier to settle your case, and only very rarely more difficult.

When business leaders have legal problems, the attorneys pick the wrong battles and fight for the wrong reasons. Creditor problems are more complicated than "you signed the contract and got the money." Partnership breakups are more complicated than "I'll keep mine, and you take yours." Unfortunately, lawyers will almost always make the wrong decision when trying to work with the other side.

The legal case is only one front in a wider war. The attorney will analyze the documents, give their opinion as to the likelihood of victory or defeat in court, and base their entire negotiation with the lender on that likelihood. A thorough understanding of the outcomes in litigation and bankruptcy is always necessary, but so is a thorough understanding of the client's financial situation, what type of creditors the client has, the availability of capital, the economics of the business, macroeconomic reality, the personalities involved,

---

[22] For a state law example, see generally *In re UPL Advisory Opinion 2003-1*, Supreme Court of Georgia, November 21, 2006. Some have construed this opinion to mean a real estate agent negotiating a short-sale residential real estate contract was engaged in UPL because in a short sale, the seller's lender negotiates the purchase price. However, the court's opinion dealt with a case in which litigation was pending, which does not occur in a normal short sale transaction.

and time. Attorneys seldom consider all of these facets of the situation.[23]

"Why should I hire a lawyer when I have no defense?"

Wars are, of course, as a rule to be avoided;
but they are far better than certain kinds of peace.

–Theodore Roosevelt

April, 2012

A bank served an $800,000 deficiency lawsuit on the owner of a construction company, regarding a shopping center lost to foreclosure. The center's occupancy dropped from 100 percent to 60 percent, and the client had used most of his cash feeding the loan after the center's rents could no longer cover the payments.

The bank showed their appreciation to the borrower for feeding the loan with personal cash for two years by refusing an extension and initiating a foreclosure as soon as the loan matured. The bank had the borrower in a vise. His business was also a tenant at the foreclosed shopping center, and thanks to a subordination agreement that didn't include a non-disturbance provision [oh, the legal malpractice stories we can tell] they could put him out of business by eviction, which because of his additional loan problems would mean bankruptcy.

It's not whether you win or lose, it's if you know what game you're playing. In most cases, both sides consider the outcome of the case on the merits a *fait accompli.* You might as well give the property back, agree to the bank's payment plan, and save all the time and stress. Right?

---

[23] Another drawback to having lawyers negotiating these cases is that the lawyer cannot talk to the other party. They can only talk to the other party's lawyer. That rule does not bind business consultants or other advisors. Advisors and the clients themselves are free to continue communicating and negotiating with the opposing party and their advisors, including their lawyer, if the opposing party is willing.

The bank's proposal to stop the litigation, though laugh-out-loud funny, wasn't unusual. If the borrower would make a $50,000 lump sum payment and sign a consent judgment for the $750,000 balance, the bank "would consider" a payment plan for the balance and postpone collection efforts. After looking at the documents, the response was 'see you in court.'

The borrower's family lawyer sent him to us, and we told the borrower he would have to hire a lawyer with expertise in foreclosure confirmation cases to defend the lawsuit. The borrower was despondent. "The bank made the loan, and we didn't pay it back. Why should I pay an attorney when we have no defense?" But we convinced him, and he reluctantly scraped together a retainer for an attorney.

Understand the attorney's role in the process. Regardless of the facts at your disposal as the defendant, make the other side prove their case. Make the adversaries do their discovery, present proper evidence, prevail on summary judgment, etc., even if the lawyer believes the adversary will prevail on the merits. Why? Doing so keeps two options open:

(1) <u>During the time of the pending litigation, something good might happen</u>. Collateral value may recover; the borrower may come into some cash to fund a settlement; a sought-after witness might be found; the plaintiff might run into financial trouble of his own; the bank might fail!

(2) <u>Maybe the lawyer is wrong</u>. Perhaps the plaintiff can't prove the case; documents can't be produced; the plaintiff's attorney may make a mistake fatal to the case; it turns out that you didn't have all the facts, or you get the right judge on the right day!

If the borrower has no money to fund litigation, then they don't have money to pay a judgment. In that case, educate the plaintiffs about the borrower's financial reality. If the borrower could fight a lawsuit but doesn't want to incur the cost, explain the very good reasons to move forward despite the odds.

Most lawyers are unwilling to do this because they are looking at the wrong big picture. They see one big picture in the sense that they see an unwinnable case and conclude that spending money defending the case isn't in their client's best interest. This advice is reasonable, but the better advice is to consider the client's entire situation and the non-legal consequences of accepting an unrealistic settlement offer or failing to defend a lawsuit, even if solely as a delaying tactic.

The lender will have the burden of proof to verify all of the elements of a basic breach of contract case. When cases do not require expensive expert consultants or witnesses, a defendant can put up a basic defense for a relatively small cost, possibly win, and create leverage to negotiate a better outcome. This is the real big picture, and most lawyers don't see it.

At the hearing, the borrower's lawyer dropped the bomb: the bank's law firm had foreclosed using the wrong legal description. The judge voided the foreclosure and requested briefs from the parties on whether he should permit the bank to re-advertise with the correct description.

The next week while we were working on our brief for the follow-up court date, the bank's attorney came to us to settle.

Engage people with what they expect; it is what they are able to discern and confirms their projections. It settles them into predictable patterns of response, occupying their minds while you wait for the extraordinary moment — that which they cannot anticipate. –Sun Tzu, The Art of War

Because our client was not in a position to borrow money or source a buyer that could close, we worked out a settlement where we let the foreclosure stand, our client escaped from the $800,000 deficiency liability, and he was able to move forward as tenants of the property on reasonable terms. This fit his goal. Putting additional capital into this asset did not make sense.

By painting the accurate financial picture for the creditors, the borrower settled his various problem loans. When the other side understood the limited cash flow of the borrower's business and the lack of unencumbered assets of the guarantor (i.e., our client), the creditors' attorneys became the ones advising their client that the cost of litigation wasn't justified. A judgment would be uncollectible and only lead to yet more expense in bankruptcy court.

The legal merits of the case are important, but the legal merits are nowhere near as vital as the borrower's ability to pay.

Understand that a borrower will accept a settlement offer even if they could never perform its terms. An attorney is unwise to recommend agreeing to a settlement without thoroughly understanding the financial picture of the borrower's business and their personal financial situation:

- accurate financial statements (a balance sheet and income statement) both year-to-date and historical
- reliable income projections going forward
- an accurate picture of asset values and liabilities, secured and unsecured
- a complete understanding of the likely outcomes in each type of bankruptcy situation

Accurate information and a clear presentation of this picture to the other side is essential. All civil disputes are about money, not law; the merits of the legal case are but one front in a complicated battle involving business, finance, communication, law, history and psychology.

The attorney does the client a disservice by allowing the client to agree to a bad settlement offer (one which the client can't reasonably expect to fulfill) to avoid or end a lawsuit. Even when convinced that a case can't be won, the better advice is to fight on rather than kick the can down the road with an impossible settlement (whether the client wants it or not).

A Lawyer Spine Installation

That the lender will never make a proposal isn't literally true. The lender will make proposals, but they will be so far out of the realm of the possible that they aren't real offers. The bank makes these proposals in the hope of catching an "I just want all of this to go away" borrower at the right time.

August, 2010

The son of a wealthy New Orleans developer had a real estate investment that was collateral for a $25 million loan to a regional bank. When the loan was made he had significant wealth, but everything had changed for the worse. We advised his lawyers on strategy to defend his interests.

He made every payment on time, but when his loan came up for renewal, the lender wanted a $10 million principal reduction, which was not possible.

The client had significant diversified interests in operating companies, real estate, and venture capital investments. He made significant equity investments, personally guaranteed loans on the vast majority of them, and was running out of cash. With respect to his largest investment, a delay in the required regulatory approvals, significant cost overruns, and litigation with former partners had stalled the company's push to profitability and was requiring a cash infusion. He also had overhead to run his offices, pay management, etc. Overall, his business of managing all of these investments had become a net user of cash rather than a provider of cash.

The lender did not want the shopping center loan to default, and applied the pressure. Our research showed, as expected, that the bank was in trouble, and this was a particularly large relationship for them. If the borrower defaulted on one loan, the bank would have to also classify as 'distressed' the many other loans at the bank that the borrower guaranteed.

In trying to get additional collateral, they demanded that he pledge his equity in an investment, which was financed by a municipal bond, knowing that doing so would violate the covenants of the bond. They also proposed that his wealthy father liquidate assets to pay their loan and also personally guarantee the loan on behalf of his son.

After several months of rearranging the deck chairs on this sinking ship of a negotiation, the bank filed a lawsuit. We ran into a problem as the litigation entered the discovery phase, and we decided to subpoena the CEO of the bank for a deposition on the case.

Our client's attorney initially refused to depose the CEO. The CEO was well known and respected as a business leader in the state. In his opinion, the bank would object to the deposition notice as frivolous and sent solely for harassment (which in many other cases was true). He thought that the court would look unfavorably on the client.

The real reason the attorney wouldn't depose the CEO was because the attorney was more worried about his own reputation than winning the case.

> *You have enemies? Good. That means you've*
> *stood up for something, sometime in your life.*
> –Winston Churchill

Ordinarily this sort of move would be seen as frivolous or a sign of desperation or being contentious, but this time was different. The CEO was on the loan committee that approved the loan, and we suspected that he knew about conflict of interest issues related to other members of the loan committee and their relationship with our client. We also had other reasons to think that the bank shouldn't have made this loan and wanted to explore them.

This wouldn't be enough to win the case, but we thought the CEO's testimony would give us negotiating leverage with the bank or, at the very least, eat up large chunks of time while the bank's attorneys fought to quash the subpoena.

After weeks of debate, the attorney agreed to send the deposition notice for the CEO. Later that same day, the bank's attorney called our client's attorney suggesting a meeting to discuss settlement.

We entered into an agreement with the bank wherein the bank forgave about one-third of the principal balance and restructured the loan for a three-year renewal term with payments that the project's cash flow could support. The project could attract more tenants with lower rents as a result of the reduced loan-to-value and debt service coverage.

Chapter 20

Making the Plaintiff Prove its Case is Your Civic Duty

February, 2012

A family-owned business, grown from nothing by European immigrants, thrived for many years. As in many family businesses, when the parents retired, the son took over. He managed to keep the business afloat through the Financial Crisis; however, in 2010, their bank failed, and a bank purchased all of the loans in a loss-share transaction with the FDIC.

Unfortunately, to weather the economy, the son signed unfavorable extensions. Not only were the payment obligations draining his business of capital, the associated real estate was several million dollars underwater. With the business as his only real asset, losing it would mean starting over with nothing. Thus began a two-year struggle to save a family business whose owners had nowhere else to go.

The new lender showed no inclination to work with the business and did not care about our client's business staying alive. The asset manager's plan, which he plainly told us, was to foreclose on the company's real estate, shut down the business, and wait for real estate values to improve before selling the property. Our client did not want to lose the property, but because he was not bankable, our strategies were limited.

Fortunately, the bank filed a lawsuit against the company, as well as the son and his parents on their personal guarantees. This was great news! The client didn't understand. "I'm being sued personally for millions of dollars, and you think that's great news?"

The lawsuit gave us breathing room. Even if we offered no defense, the case would take six months or so of time. And we had a few issues that we could assert as counterclaims. Perhaps the court would dismiss them, but that process would give us another two to four months for the bank to file a motion and the court to rule.

A few months into the litigation, the client's attorney called with more "bad" news. We had requested that the bank produce its appraisals of the property through discovery, and the bank's attorney was objecting to their production.

We could scarcely believe our luck. "Discovery dispute? Awesome. That'll eat up six months to a year." We would have to file a motion to compel the production of the appraisals, which we were virtually certain we would win.

The law was crystal clear: the bank had to produce the appraisals in litigation. The attorney wanted to send an abusive litigation letter (which would allege that the motion was frivolous and requests that the court sanction the client and his lawyer) demanding that the bank withdraw their objection. "No! Don't do that! They'll withdraw the motion, and the discovery period will resume. We need the time."

Several months passed, and we prevailed on the motion. The bank produced the appraisals, which were terribly inaccurate and inflated. While not unexpected, this was bad news. The inflated value in the appraisal would make it more difficult for the bank to agree to a workable settlement. Fortunately, the bank's lawyers took their sweet time filing a summary judgment motion, but they eventually did. After 18 months of litigation, we reassessed our situation.

Since our delay tactics began, two fortunate things had occurred. First, the son's business had improved significantly. Second, the bank had a new appraisal closer to market value. Taken together, we analyzed the company's likely result if it filed for bankruptcy reorganization. The company filed, and the lawsuit was suspended.[24]

After consulting with the client's bankruptcy attorney and prevailing on several key motions in bankruptcy court, we returned to the lender with a new settlement offer. Because the bank was a loss share bank, we structured a proposal that we knew would be more appealing than continuing the court battles.

The bank agreed to accept 50 cents on the dollar, let our client keep the property, and gave the guarantors two years to finance the payoff while making monthly payments on the loan that the business's cash flow could support. This settlement achieved all of our client's goals: keep the property, continue his business, end the lawsuit, and give him time to repair his credit and become bankable again.

"Call Us Back When Your Bank Fails."

March, 2011

A husband and wife owned a successful manufacturing business and had invested much of their profits into various partnerships investing in real estate. They were also friends of ours. The husband had guaranteed two projects along with a wealthy man. The wealthy man was now penniless, and the bank wanted our friend to pay down the loan significantly. After researching his case, we gave him very unusual advice. We told him not to agree to anything and to call us back when the bank fails.

Looking at the bank's financials, we knew the bank was finished. It was only a matter of time. And he was not able to comply with the asset manager's demands for large principal pay downs. We told him to wait.

---

[24] When the operating company files for reorganization, any lawsuits in state court are suspended. However, the lender can and sometimes will make a motion in state court to proceed against the guarantors personally. The guarantors will have a hard time defeating this motion, and if granted the bank can proceed with that litigation and have the court rule on summary judgment against the guarantors personally. When looking out at the horizon and seeing a potential bankruptcy for the operating company, paint the proper picture of the guarantor's financial situation and the likelihood of the bank collecting a judgment against the guarantor, which will hopefully dissuade the bank from trying to re-open the litigation against the guarantors.

Sure enough, almost exactly a year later the FDIC closed the bank, and a new bank took over. We were engaged and made a settlement proposal to the new asset manager based upon the values, cash flow, and poor financial state of our client's personal finances.

Unfortunately, this bank wasn't fooling around. Within weeks he was served with a lawsuit demanding almost $10 million on his personal guarantee. They also aggressively exercised their right to take all of the rents that the tenants of one of the projects were paying.

This move by the bank was idiotic. Why do a rental assignment on residential condos-turned-apartments? Many of the tenants will move out because they don't understand what the rental assignment is or, in a commercial setting, fear the property will be foreclosed and sold on the cheap by the bank. The assignment probably gives any credit tenant the right to terminate the lease and move out. The upside of a little cash to the bank doesn't justify the damage these rent assignments cause—a lender liability cause of action should exist in these circumstances because the lender is doing the rent assignment for the main purpose of squeezing the borrowers while killing the collateral value.

We recommended counsel to represent them in the litigation and continued settlement negotiations. The new lender wouldn't budge. We had to wait.

We also analyzed the situation at the property and realized that Chapter 11 reorganization was a real possibility. The client hired bankruptcy counsel and filed on the borrower entities that owned the property. The lender still wouldn't budge. We had to wait.

After about a year of litigation, the lender prevailed on a summary judgment motion in the lawsuit. The lender would not negotiate a settlement of the bankruptcy case. They would only agree to settlements that weren't possible. Our client was supremely frustrated that this was taking so long, but we could not agree to a settlement that was impossible to perform. We had to wait.

Eventually, the lender agreed to a settlement proposal, but between the internal bank approval process, back-and-forth negotiation on the details of the settlement agreement, and other unnecessary delays, several more months passed.

The case settled, at about 50 cents on the dollar, two and a half years after the bank failed. The even more frustrating part was that the final settlement was only slightly different, maybe a few tens of thousands of dollars, from our original offer when the bank first failed. If there isn't the ability to perform the sort of settlement that the bank demands, letting the time pass is the best option.

Making the Lender Prove Damages

Often the lender cannot give you a precise number as to what amount is owed at a given point in time, nor can they account for how they applied any prior payments or collected sums to the balance owed. This may provide a means by which the attorney can attack the judgment or prevail, at least temporarily, in a bank's summary judgment motion. Again, make the bank prove its case.

In many cases, the bank's counsel had the bank officer state the amount owed in a deposition, and the lawyer used this testimony in his summary judgment motion for the bank to prove damages. But in one of our cases, the court denied the summary judgment because our client's lawyer argued that without documentation, the proof offered wasn't sufficient. Although the bank's attorney re-filed and provided the documents, the process afforded our client many months of delay, and the case eventually settled several months after the bank obtained a judgment against our client.

Chapter 21

Do Not Threaten. Do.

August, 2011

An investor owned a minority ownership interest in a shopping center. After netting out the operating expenses, the shopping center was still covering the interest and principal every month on the loan. But when the loan was up for renewal, the lender would not renew or extend. The bank filed suit against the guarantors, electing not to foreclose.

> *This is another situation where the creditor doesn't want the collateral because the market for it was nonexistent. If values have plummeted, taking the collateral becomes a cost and does nothing to get the bad loan off the bank's books. And in this case the asset manager again thought collecting against the guarantor would be a snap. But again, the originating bank's underwriting did in the special assets collector.*

The partnership already obtained counsel who, unfortunately, had not provided any real defenses and also threatened the bank with counterclaims

165

but never followed through. This only made the situation more contentious.

Never threaten anything you cannot or will not do. This was the lawyer's first mistake, which soured the relationship. Threats without action are more damaging than unsuccessful action. Why? Respect. When you don't follow through, you look weak (and probably are) and also like a liar trying to bluff and BS your way out of trouble. Acting this way makes the other side hate you because you are wasting their time.

Humble words and increased preparations are signs that the enemy is about to advance. Violent language and driving forward as if to the attack are signs that he will retreat. –Sun Tzu, The Art of War

Threatening and following through won't make the other side love you, but they will respect you as long as your defenses or counterclaims aren't frivolous. Frivolous claims do no good even when made for the purpose of delay because they will anger the other side and make them more aggressive, which will speed up, not delay, the process.

All of that said, threatening is largely a waste of effort. Do not threaten. Do. Generally, threats are not well received and have little impact. Surprise multiplies the impact of the act, be it bankruptcy, counterclaims or an act in response to an aggressive collector/lender.

Most people in these situations want to avoid conflict and work together on a payment plan. Creditors pursue aggressively through official channels while the person in contact with the borrower soothes them with "the devil made me do it" type statements such as, "It's just standard procedure." You should do the same thing in defending lawsuits, filing bankruptcy, etc.

Do your best to keep everyone calm and going through the process. Professionals in the collections business want calm discussions as well unless the debtor does something to make it personal, and the quickest way to make it personal is to get caught lying or making threats, particularly threats with which you have no intention of following through.

But if the other side wants to fight, you must fight as aggressively, if not more so, as the other side.

Collections efforts backfire; hilarity ensues.

The borrower didn't retain us until after his lawyer had already lost the case, and his client had a judgment against him. One of the lender's remedies in most real estate cases is that upon a default, the lender may exercise an 'assignment of rents' to notify the tenants that the mortgage is in default and furthermore that going forward they should send their rent payments to the lender instead of the landlord/borrower. This is usually a mistake.

The lender exercised their assignment of the rents of the tenants at the shopping center, so the tenants paid the rent directly to the bank. However, in the lender's hubris against the wealthy borrower, they refused to cover any of the cost of operating the property, which they were entitled to do under the loan documents. The lender expected the borrower to continue to do that, and he was not in any position to cover these costs.

These tactics backfired on the lender when the tenants threatened constructive eviction and gave notice they were moving out. This would severely impact the value of the property.

We instruct clients that if the lender isn't providing cash to cover operations, do not cover them out of pocket, even though the loan documents probably require it. Although not maintaining the property is an event of default, the borrower is already in default in this situation. Causing another default doesn't matter when the lender is already exercising its remedies on another loan default.

It sends a message and often provides hilarity. A businessman owned an apartment building in rural South Georgia, and a bank in Minnesota acquired his bank. The bank exercised the rental assignment, and we instructed the client not to spend any money out of his own pocket for repairs and maintenance.

A few days later the asset manager called from Minnesota. She angrily demanded that our client maintain the property, preserve their collateral, etc. We explained that the client had no personal cash with which to do so. As the call wrapped up she added, "And your client sent all of the tenants a letter instructing them to direct any questions and issues to me—now my phone is blowing up. A woman called this morning demanding that I fix her stove."

We hadn't asked the client to send out the letters, but we loved it. We were planning on the client filing for bankruptcy reorganization, and because the bank exercised the rental assignment, we could blame everything on them. The case settled two months later.

With a summary judgment in place and the bank attempting collection procedures, we helped assemble financial information to show the asset manager why the bank needed to settle. Our problem was a familiar one: the borrower had considerable assets, which were all protected in trusts. Losing millions in real estate did not affect his lifestyle at all. This irked the asset manager. We had to advise the client—force him—to change his behavior. Stay out of the country club. Stop driving around in a $90,000 SUV.

The lender demanded that the borrower force distributions from the trusts to pay off the loan. We explained and showed them that this wasn't an option because of the trust documents and particularly because the borrower was not the sole beneficiary of the trust. That money wasn't going anywhere.

Meanwhile, the parties negotiated an interim agreement where the operating costs of the property were taken out of the collected rents that the bank was getting. But the tenants were still threatening to vacate, and the lender was nervous.[25]

Eventually we satisfied the asset manager that collections efforts would be fruitless. But even in those situations, the lender isn't going to give up and go away. The borrower has to sacrifice something for the bank to save face. The asset manager needs a scalp to get the deal through committee.

Even though nobody ever hears about these workouts (or cares for that matter), the bank worries about how it looks to imaginary others and how it might embolden other borrowers to want the same deal, which is idiotic but

---

[25] That we might have suggested and encouraged said tenants to do so is theoretically possible, at least in theory.

how this works. Any settlement agreement will contain a confidentiality clause with harsh penalties for disclosure of the terms therein, so the bank doesn't have much to worry about in reality.[26]

But also in reality, the bank will demand that the borrower take some pain out of ego and jealousy. But when the time comes to make a deal, you make a deal—the lender was at its furthest point, in our opinion, and the client would part with the small cash payment to conclude the matter and have the home front return to normal.

The bank eventually accepted a settlement wherein the client handed over the property and made a small cash payment (well, small for this client). In the end, the bank settled at about 50 cents on the dollar, which is a great result for a loan involving income producing property. From the bank's standpoint, the rents from the property would mitigate their losses further, and from the borrower's standpoint, had decided to exit the real estate business, which the settlement accomplished.

Responding to Threats

We've seen all kinds of stunts to try to get a payment, such as threatening lawsuits, serving the suit on the wife, making cumbersome document requests, suing people who aren't under any obligation to pay, etc. You must never react to an aggressive move by the other side by increasing the offer. Doing so will embolden the other side to be more aggressive because last time it worked.

---

[26] Confidentiality of a settlement can be a problem in situations wherein the borrower gives the lender a consent judgment as security for performance of the terms of the settlement. The lender would only enforce the consent judgment in the event of an uncured default, but after the settlement, the borrower many seek financing, which may be unrelated to the prior case, and the new lender may discover the consent judgment if the old lender recorded it. The borrower is then between a rock and a hard place: he cannot explain to the new lender how the judgment is not enforceable, the payment terms of the settlement, etc., because doing so would violate the confidentiality provisions of the settlement. The old lender won't consent to disclosure of the settlement terms to the new lender. Therefore, make sure any settlement agreement with a consent judgment feature provides that the consent judgment may not be filed in the public records absent an uncured event of default by the borrower.

If you must respond, respond by changing your settlement proposal for the worse. For instance, if a lender files a lawsuit, you might have to cut the offer because now that the bank sued the borrower personally, the lender funding the settlement payment has withdrawn their loan commitment.

Chapter 22

Going on Offense - Capitalizing on a Lack of Attention to Detail

Creating a Prisoner's Dilemma in Multiple-Creditor Situations

> *Prisoner's Dilemma: a paradox in decision analysis in which two parties acting in their own best interest pursue a course of action that does not result in the ideal outcome. The prisoner's dilemma is set in such a way that both parties choose to protect themselves at the expense of the other participant. As a result of following a purely logical thought process to help oneself, both participants find themselves in a worse state than if they had cooperated with each other in the decision-making process.*

Fortunately for borrowers with multiple loan problems, privacy laws prevent lenders from discussing their borrower's loans or financial condition with third parties, including other creditors. Yes, limited exceptions to this rule exist but not in the case we are discussing here. Creditors do not conspire against borrowers because in distressed situations, everyone knows the debtor has only a limited amount of assets. The creditors are adverse and don't trust one another any more than they trust the debtor.

March, 2013

The borrower faced a difficult employment situation and multiple loan problems, and we had been engaged to assist his attorney. The borrower's employer was downsizing, and he was laid off from the sales force. Through freelancing he was able to make about 40 percent of his prior salary. His decline in income made it difficult for him to continue making payments on two ill-advised real estate investments. And unfortunately for him, the lender on vacant land in a failed vacation resort project, "Z Bank", also held the mortgage on his home. We were able to use this problem to our advantage.

The lender on the other real estate investment in which he was involved, a tract of land in South Carolina, was a large regional bank, "Bank B". He had been making the payments, but we knew it was good money after bad. The borrower had to stop making payments because he could no longer afford it. The value of the land was 20 percent of the outstanding loan balance.

Two months after we advised the borrower to stop paying, Bank B made contact, and we spent an additional four months going through a frustrating process of explaining and substantiating the borrower's lack of liquidity, other loan problems, lawsuits, severe income decline, and other personal issues. We were getting nowhere.

But after six months, two things happened: We received a short sale offer for only slightly less than Bank B's appraised value (the land had been on the market for two and a half years with no offers at any price). Bank B wanted a consent judgment against our client for the remaining outstanding balance on the loan in exchange for approving the short sale, which was a deal killer. However, a day or two later the court set a hearing date in the lawsuit Z Bank had filed against the borrower. The court would consider Z Bank's motion for summary judgment in 5 weeks.

We quickly contacted Bank B and explained that the short sale had to occur before the hearing because the court was sure to grant Z Bank's motion for summary judgment. Z Bank would have a judgment for many times Bank

B's loan (and many times the borrower's net worth). If Z Bank put a judgment lien on the South Carolina property before the sale, the borrower could not sell the property to the buyer or anyone else. Bank B would have to foreclose to extinguish the judgment lien, which in South Carolina means judicial foreclosure, which meant months of delay and expense even if the borrower didn't contest the foreclosure, which we regretted to inform Bank B he surely would.

Therefore, we proposed that the borrower would go through with the short sale, but only if Bank B forgave the entire deficiency. We argued that any recovery on that judgment would be more than offset by their expenses, and their judgment would be a fraction of the judgment Z Bank was sure to obtain.

Meanwhile, we contacted Z Bank and advised them that Bank B required a consent judgment to approve a short sale of its collateral and that the parties (the buyer and seller) set a closing date before the summary judgment would be final, such that Bank B could put its judgment lien on the property mortgaged to Z Bank and prevent its sale absent a foreclosure, which we happened to know Z Bank did not want to do because no properties in the area had sold in years.

We were offering 80 percent of Z Bank's appraised value, sourced from a family member willing to loan the client the funds. We suggested to Z Bank's asset manager that they take the offer quickly.[27] If accepted, Z Bank would take a huge loss on this loan, but we argued that the property was worth about half of the appraised value. Z Bank would obtain a better recovery by accepting our proposal.

Thus, the two banks have a prisoner's dilemma: if they both take the settlements, they both get cash and resolve their loan. But if Z Bank takes a settlement and Bank B doesn't, Bank B can put a lien on what other assets the man owned, which were encumbered by loans but had considerable equity, and get a far better recovery. On the other hand, if Bank B takes a settlement and Z Bank doesn't settle, Z Bank will have a lien on the equity in the other properties and get a far better recovery. And neither creditor knows what the other creditor will do.

---

[27] Very quickly, indeed, before the family member came to her senses about loaning money to a family member. Seriously, we made that point to the bank.

We wanted both to settle, but if only one settled, we would consider it a successful, though temporary, result. We could negotiate with the one remaining bank and reach a settlement. What kept us awake at night was if both banks refused to settle. The client would be crestfallen and might be persuaded into his lawyer's advice to file for personal bankruptcy in advance of the summary judgment hearing.

Although sometimes bankruptcy a good idea, in this case the borrower had liquid assets that would be protected somewhat from a judgment creditor but definitely on the table in bankruptcy. We saw taking our chances negotiating on the judgment as the less bad course of action.

We expected the potential payoff would focus the creditors on the reality of the situation—the borrower has a contract on the property and the buyer (for Bank B) and the family member (for Z Bank) have proof of funds. Resolution is no longer abstraction discussed in weekly meetings.

Thankfully, Bank B agreed to the deal. The bank swept away the usual approval process, which usually takes months, and in five weeks the short sale closed, and Bank B forgave the entire deficiency.

That Bank B was a financially healthy super-regional bank made it easier for them to forgive the deficiency, and we had provided mountains of information explaining the borrower's financial situation and showing that the appraised value was not realistic.

Meanwhile, Z Bank rejected our offer initially and demanded a deficiency judgment as well. But with cajoling, a few concessions, and a payment plan on an additional part of the deficiency, we reached a settlement. Usually these negotiations would take a couple of months to negotiate, paper up, and close, but this one moved quickly because we presented the consent judgment for Bank B as a done deal—that the property was under contract for short sale and that the borrower would execute a consent judgment at closing.

Nobody at Z Bank asked the right question, which was whether the borrower had *agreed* to the consent judgment on the deficiency. We didn't have to tell Z Bank that giving Bank B a consent judgment was a deal killer. But if Z Bank asked that specific question, we would have to admit that we were still negotiating the issue and retreated to saying that he would do it only if Z Bank didn't take the deal. The bank would've gotten testy.

Furthermore, nobody at Z Bank ever asked us why in the world our client would agree to give Bank B the consent judgment for the entire deficiency. They did not put themselves in the borrower's shoes.

This case involved more than a few sleepless nights given what was at stake, but in the end, we were fairly confident that each would act in its own self-interest, which was to confess, i.e., settle.

Bankruptcy as an Offensive Weapon

November, 2014

A loan officer at a community bank contacted us, and he had a big problem. One of his customers, to whom the bank had loaned millions of dollars, was in deep trouble. The customer's business was a popular catering company and event space in a coastal resort community, and another bank had a loan against the company's property that was about to mature.

The lender would not negotiate any sort of extension that the borrower could perform, and the company was in arrears on property and payroll tax payments. Therefore, the loan officer's bank could not loan the customer any more money, and he did not think any other lenders would, either. The building was old, with considerable deferred maintenance issues, and the value was not there.

The loan officer had learned that the lender had just advertised the property for foreclosure. The company's revenue was seasonal, and the business was in its slow part of the year. Also, the company was short of cash, which it needed to make purchases for upcoming events.

Customers had already put down deposits for events many months in advance. If the bank took their property, they would have to cancel all of the events and risk being sued by their customers. A foreclosure would put them out of business. Their lender would not cooperate unless the loan was paid down far more than any cash they had or could source.[28]

---

[28] *The lender in this case had acquired a local bank from whom the company had borrowed the money. The acquiring bank and its counsel were in collections mode—they wanted to liquidate all of the bank's problem loans as quickly as possible and had no regard for the borrower or his company.*

We attempted to educate the lender on the ramifications of foreclosing on the property, which would mean that the loan's personal guarantor, the owner of the business, would not only lose their source of income but would file personal bankruptcy. When all else failed, we assisted our client in hiring bankruptcy counsel and filed for Chapter 11 reorganization the day before the foreclosure auction. We had stopped the bleeding, but we did not have a strong case.

The bankruptcy filing gave us a little breathing room to further attempt to find a refinancing source. During this time, we tried to demonstrate to the asset manager that a settlement would be far preferable to foreclosing on the property, which was worth well less than the loan, and ruining the income of their only guarantor. Meanwhile, bankruptcy counsel on both sides filed motions and attended contentious hearings.

After many weeks passed, we caught a break. We realized that the original bank that made the loan did not have a subordination agreement with the tenant, and the tenant leased the property prior to the bank's loan (and mortgage). The bankrupt entity owned the real estate and leased the property to a separate entity comprising the business. With the lease not subordinated to the bank's mortgage, the bank would not have the right to evict the company after the foreclosure.

This case was another example of lawyer myopia. When we mentioned this to our client's attorney, she responded correctly, "Even if the mortgage isn't subordinate, the lease is in default, or soon will be in default after the foreclosure. The bank can just do a dispossessory. And if the bank confirms the foreclosure and gets a judgment against the guarantor, he'll have to file for bankruptcy and the company is out of business." True, but irrelevant.

The primary objective in the early stage of the case was to delay the foreclosure long enough to have the events for which customers had already paid deposits. Therefore, even if the bank prevailed on their motion to lift the bankruptcy stay and foreclose on the property, the dispossessory process would give the client another two to three months of the coming year, which could make a huge difference in the outcome.

Also, having another issue to fight about gives the lender another issue to think about, and additional unfavorable outcomes to worry about. The bank lawyers and other creditor lawyers are just as pessimistic, if not more than any other lawyer (being predominately housed in large law firms), so they will paint the worst-case scenario to the asset manager, which helps our case. Unfortunately, that advantage cuts both ways, as we have seen repeatedly.

The bankruptcy attorney had prevailed against all of the bank's initial motions but was concerned about an upcoming hearing. The attorney told us we should settle the case, if at all possible, prior to the hearing because she thought the court would rule in the bank's favor, ending the case. But by this time, the busy season had arrived, and the client needed less time to finish all of the events. Other than having the events, the client was happy to give the property back to the bank—the building needed a full renovation, which the client could not afford.

We conceded on the issue of the back taxes (which had caused the state to place liens on the property), and the asset manager conceded on the issue of a few more months before the borrower had to move out, and the cases settled before the hearing date. The bank agreed to let the borrower stay in the building until all of the reserved events had taken place.

The bank agreed to release the personal guarantee, finally realizing that the guarantor by that time had nothing they could collect. Many months later, the bank sold the property for about 70 percent of the loan balance, which meant that the guarantor escaped almost $1 million in liability on the deficiency.

It was a big win. The client kept its existing customers happy and ended up finding an even better location, with better space, and with rent for less than its old mortgage payments. He also escaped considerable liability on the deficiency. The loan officer friend who referred the company to us wouldn't need to put this customer in default of his bank's loans. Also, the settlement right-sized the borrower's balance sheet, making him and his company bankable again.

Chapter 23

Going on Offense - Taking Advantage of Bureaucratic Failures

Bureaucracies tend to make fewer mistakes overall because the focus is always on process and not results. But when a bureaucracy does make a mistake, it's usually a doozy.

The opportunity to secure ourselves against defeat lies in our own hands, but the opportunity of defeating the enemy is provided by the enemy himself.

−Sun Tzu, The Art of War

May, 2012

Our client had made a bad real estate deal, the loan was in default, and the property was next to worthless. The lender in question had made many bad real estate loans, and by regulation had written down the value of the collateral (the borrower's property) to the appraised value on the bank's internal books. Even so, the bank's appraisal was significantly higher than the actual value, there being no demand for land, which was preventing a settlement.

Then a funny thing happened. The bank erroneously sent out incorrect monthly statements to every one of their borrowers that showed not the actual balance owed on the loan, but the written-down value that the bank carried for the loan on its internal books. The client happened to have access to enough cash, and the number was around 30 percent of what he owed. He called the bank requesting a payoff and persuaded the person at the bank to send him an email confirming the payoff at the lower number, which she did. He promptly wired the "payment in full" to the bank.

The asset manager was none the wiser and never even heard about the payment, until he heard about it from the bank's lawyer. When a loan is paid off, the bank is obligated by state law to release the mortgage within a certain period, 30 to 60 days, so as not to unfairly encumber property on the record in which they no longer have a security interest.

Having received a payoff letter and sent the bank that amount, the borrower waited out the allotted time for the bank to cancel the mortgage on the record, which of course the bank did not do. When the statutory period expired, the borrower sued the bank for specific performance, i.e., to file a release of the mortgage in the real estate records, as well as damages to which he was entitled under the statute.

When the bank's lawyer informed the asset manager of this development, he went ballistic. The bank filed a motion to dismiss the case, threatened to file motions to sanction the plaintiff and his attorney, etc., but the bank lost. Eventually, the case settled before trial almost 18 months later.

What was our client's chance of prevailing at trial? One never knows. However, the lender could not afford to lose this case; statements with the incorrect and lower loan balances were sent to every borrower whose loan was impaired. Other borrowers could pay off the lower balance, potentially, and argue collateral estoppel[29] prevents the bank from re-litigating the issue.

---

[29] *Collateral Estoppel* prevents a party from re-litigating determinations on issues made in prior actions. The determination may be an issue of fact or an issue of law. If the bank

Read the Documents. Make them pay.

November, 2009

A man owned an operating business earning seven figures in net profit annually. His bank failed, and the FDIC sold his loan to a small, out of state bank. Our intelligence work on the new bank led us to believe that the new bank bought the loan in a pool at a significant discount. This small bank informed the client they would not be renewing the loan, which matured a few months from that point.

The business was related to commodities, but its profits were highly inelastic. Despite the steady income, credit conditions at the time were so tight that he could not borrow enough to pay off the loan. Assuming that the good times would continue forever, the client was cash poor, having invested in bad real estate deals and living beyond his means. Cash reserves were low.

He had already called several of the regional, bigger banks that had sought his business in the past. While they all wanted to lend him money, they were only willing to lend 50 cents on the dollar for his receivables, factoring out certain smaller accounts. He owed over $4 million, and the banks would loan only $2 million. The lending criteria had changed. He could not borrow what he owed.

Our first task is to read and understand the documents, and these documents provided an incredible gift. The section on advances on the line of credit provided "so long as borrower is not in default under this agreement and has otherwise complied with the covenants and agreements, herein, lender shall fund advances on the loan in the manner provided..."

Lender "shall" fund. Such a provision is highly unusual. In loan documents for lines of credit, the provisions, if not heavily negotiated, will provide essentially that the bank can fund or not fund a draw request at its own discretion, and the borrower can't do anything about it. This provision was the opposite.

---

lost the case to our client, another court would accept our court's ruling as binding on their court and the parties. This is true even if the subsequent actions are in different courts or even different states. Judgments of state courts are given preclusive effect in other state and federal courts under the Full Faith and Credit Clause of the U.S. Constitution.

Armed with this knowledge, the client sent in a $1 million draw request for the open amount on the line of credit. The bank denied the draw request as expected. "We don't have to fund that. We bought that loan from the FDIC." This gave the client a cause of action for breach of contract. His lawyers sued the bank in federal court for specific performance and asked for an expedited hearing.

This bank's president bought the loan thinking it would make a quick payday by forcing our client to cough up the cash. Instead, they received a two-by-four to the backside. The bank's attorney called to schedule a settlement conference immediately. After a few shouting matches, the bank's lawyer was able to explain to his client that the documents bound them to perform (unless they settled). And once the bank understood the nature of the client's business, they agreed to a settlement where our client paid just over $2 million to settle a $4 million of outstanding debt.

We emphasized that if the bank chose to foreclose, their collateral was his receivables, which were tens of thousands of consumer receivables with small balances. The bank was not in a position to operate the business and it would be difficult to sell, operating exclusively in a highly regulated industry. If our client filed for bankruptcy, the bank would be on the losing end of the situation.

Who won this case? Everybody involved in the case won. Our client wiped $2 million from the liabilities on his company's balance sheet. The payoff of the loan was many times what the bank paid to purchase the loan; they discounted the loan payoff but still made off like bandits. The professionals were paid. The employees of the client's company still had jobs.

Who lost the case? (1) The stockholders of the failed bank. (2) All bank customers, who indirectly pay for the banks' increased deposit insurance premiums as a result of the bank failing and the financial crisis generally. (3) Ultimately you lost, Dear Taxpayer, because you ultimately pay the bank bailouts and any shortfall in the FDIC deposit insurance fund, either in the form of your tax dollars directly, or indirectly as interest payments on the ever-expanding national debt.

The client borrowed the payoff from a regional bank. After the old loan was settled, this bank, and every other bank in town, was willing to lend him double what they originally committed. From the lender's perspective, they

182

were looking at the company's balance sheet with a greatly reduced amount of debt. Unfortunately for those banks, our client was not interested in borrowing anything more after the near-death experience he had been through.

Chapter 24

The One Thing

Real courage is when you know you're licked before you begin, but you begin anyway and see it through no matter what.

–Harper Lee

Maria's life experiences give her perspective. She is a proud woman, and deservedly so, having raised a son and daughter through difficult times and providing for the family during her husband's illness and decline. She has her own small business doing what she loves. Her daughter recently earned a degree at the local technical college. Her son returned to California and is doing better than ever. I asked Maria, "what's the best piece of advice you can give to people dealing with financial ruin?"

"Having someone who will just listen can be very powerful. Keeping everything a secret makes you feel isolated, while at the same time you feel ostracized despite nobody knowing what you are enduring. If no one knows you need help, how can anyone provide help? Being open about your life and your fears kills the fear's power over you, because the fear controls you when you want to hide from everything else. You also are reminded that you are not alone, and you don't have to go it alone."

• • • • •

From a December 14, 2015 story in The Guardian (UK) about oil & gas workers in the Alberta, Canada oilfields, where 40,000 jobs have been lost since the 2015 oil price collapse:

"There's a lot of isolation and feeling like they're not engaged in real life," *says Angela Angel, a corporate consultant and sociologist who wrote master thesis on mental well-being of male mobile workers in the resource sector.*

Angel conducted her studies during the recession [that accompanied the 2008-09 Financial Crisis], when the price of oil collapsed suddenly to $40 a barrel and more than half of Alberta oil & gas workers were laid off, exacerbating many addiction and financial struggles.

It wasn't the financial crisis that motivated her research, however, but the loss of her older brother, an oil and gas worker who killed himself in 2007. He was 35.

Angel, whose father also worked in the oil patch, describes Jason as "the Alberta boy," a hard-working truck driver who loved his job despite the long hours and days away from his wife and two sons. "The company he worked for, part of their culture was using crack cocaine to work longer shifts and longer hours."

Soon Jason isolated himself from loved ones. "That was really the start of the downfall for him," she says. "We thought that he was getting better because he was becoming more communicative, but we know that when someone becomes suicidal they start to have a more positive outlook because they have a plan."

When her family buried him, staff at the funeral chapel told her that services for five other young men had recently been held, all suicides at the height of the boom.

⁙ ⁙ ⁙ ⁙ ⁙

Between January and June [2015], suicides spiked 30% compared to 2014. At this rate, 654 Albertans will have killed themselves this year, an unprecedented number for a region that already had the second highest suicide rates amongst the 10 provinces. Only Saskatchewan, another energy-dependent region, has a higher rate, and it's seen 19% more suicides this year.[30]

What shall we conclude from all of these stories, all of this information, and all of this advice? What you could learn is more important than knowing when to stop making payments, or knowing "you don't increase your settlement offer if they file a lawsuit," or remembering to stash your Ferrari at a covered garage in Reno if the bank gets a judgment. For instance, you could learn:

- *Fear of failing is why people don't succeed.* Don't base your actions on avoiding failure. Instead, prepare for how you will deal with failing, then forget about failing and base all of your actions on succeeding.
- *What people advise you to do and what would actually help you rarely coincide.*
- *The more critical the deadline, the more likely you get voicemail at the help desk.* Put another way, when you rush and hurry, Go!

---

[30] *The boom, the bust, the darkness: suicide rate soars in wake of Canada's oil crisis.* By Omar Mouallem, The Guardian (UK), December 14, 2015.

Go! Go!, everything takes longer, takes more effort, and you get poorer results.[31]

While those lessons are important, this social psychology principle controls the entire process:

When a person is in a situation,
he will attribute
his actions to the situation.

However, when others observe the person
in that situation, they attribute the person's
actions to the person's character.

Do you understand the disconnect between the adverse
parties, be they debtor/creditor, divorcing business
partners, or other civil (and domestic) litigation?

The defaulting borrower looks at his situation and thinks:

The economy cratered and my customers couldn't pay me.
My business had no cash flow because of the bad weather.
My business partner was incompetent.
The project had severe construction delays and we lost big tenants.
The CFO embezzled millions of dollars.
A big chain competitor opened next door.

While the creditors look at the borrower's situation and think:

He doesn't honor his agreements. He's probably a liar, too.
She makes excuses for her lack of good business sense.
He either blames others for his mistakes or associates with crooked

---

[31] Good luck trying to explain this concept to a teenager.

people; which is it?
He thinks the rules don't apply to him.
She thinks she is better than us.
He can afford a 7-series BMW but can't pay? A liar and a cheater, that's what he is.
I still see him playing golf at the country club every Thursday. He is mocking us.

Meanwhile, the defaulting borrower looks at the creditors' situation and thinks:

They are unreasonable.
They are out of touch with reality.
This guy's an idiot.
He bullies weak people to get his way.
She will lie to get what she wants.
Her word is no good; she said they would work with me.
They have no regard for my employees or my family.

While the creditors look at their own situation and think:

We had to protect our shareholders.
You must this way when dealing with crooks.
The banker gave you his word, but the agreement wasn't reduced to writing and signed. We couldn't honor it.
The regulators/politicians/board of directors decided we had to do it this way.
I was only following orders and doing my job.
You signed the loan and got the money; we are blameless.
We lied to her about their rights, but she should've hired her own advisor.

Is it any wonder that both sides can't find common ground? Each side feels completely justified in their actions and complete contempt for the character of the opposition, no matter how many dollars are owed or at issue.

The dollar amount matters so little because these "business" disputes aren't business disputes at all. There is no such thing. All disputes, regardless of the subject matter, are *personal.*

> *"It's just business" is the quintessential justification of one's actions, while at the same time implying that the opponent is thin-skinned for being angry about the unfair outcome.*

These 'business' disputes are deeply personal, which explains why resolving them is difficult at best. The emotion is in the deal, and the parties have three choices in addressing the emotion:

- **Let out the emotion and have a screaming argument**, which is sometimes beneficial if both sides are of the same temperament, and extremely counterproductive if they are not;

- **Suppress or ignore the emotions**, which can lead to severe anxiety and irrational thought processes when a person's career or livelihood is at stake; suppressing is particularly counterproductive unless the person is accustomed to high stress and understands the process;

- *Acknowledge and admit that the situation is personal and emotionally charged—i.e., name it;* this requires *vulnerability—* someone must go first (a trait common among entrepreneurs, but rare among debt collectors and lawyers);

If you find yourself in this situation, or advising someone in this situation, the smartest thing to do or advise is to *listen to what the other side is saying.* Use the basic negotiation skill of *repeating what you heard* back to them. Understanding your opponent's *true character* is as important as understanding their perception of the *situation* upon which they are blaming their actions.

When to bring a knife to a gunfight

We had entitled one of the chapters "don't bring a knife to a gunfight," but knives are deadlier.[32] Knives are easier to use. Knives don't run out of ammunition. Knives give little warning.

The chapter is instead entitled "making the lender prove its case is your civic duty." Consider the story of *David vs. Goliath.*[33]

> *Goliath was the most fearsome warrior of the Philistines, standing twice as tall as any other man, armed with a sword, a spear, and had a javelin slung on his back. A shield and a suit of the finest bronze armor protected him. David volunteered to fight him on Israel's behalf, and King Saul replied, "You are not able to go out against this Philistine and fight him; you are only a young man, and he has been a warrior from his youth," but David convinced the king to allow him to fight.*

> *Wearing no armor and armed only with a sling and five stones, David killed Goliath with one well-placed shot to the forehead, which was the only part of Goliath's body not protected by the suit of armor. The Israelites subsequently routed the Philistine army.*

The best weapon is better than the biggest weapon. Flexibility and mobility may be of greater value than armor. Moreover, weapons must be deployed effectively. The lender may have the ability to deploy vast resources to fund endless litigation, but if they foreclose on the wrong property description, they lose. If they think a pack of New York and Atlanta big firm lawyers impresses a South Georgia bankruptcy judge, they lose. If they refuse to fund a $1 million draw request because they bought that loan from the FDIC, they lose.

Goliath assessed the situation incorrectly: he saw a boy with a piece of cloth and a rock instead of a boy who had killed lions and bears with his sling. He did not identify and protect his one weak spot. Nor did he properly deploy his weapons, leaving his javelin slung over his back. He

---

[32] Per FBI statistics, 10% of gunshot wounds are fatal, while 30% of stab wounds are fatal.
[33] 1 Samuel 17 (NIV)

employed the wrong tactics by charging directly at David, making himself an easier target.

> *Know the enemy and know yourself; in a hundred battles you will never be in peril. When you are ignorant of the enemy, but know yourself, your chances of winning or losing are equal. If ignorant both of your enemy and yourself, you are certain in every battle to be in peril. –Sun Tzu, The Art of War*

In addition to his cloth sling, his rocks, and his experience using them, David had something else. He possessed the three traits no other Israelite possessed: David *understood the enemy and himself, he had the courage to do what had to be done, and he stepped into the arena.* All of the weapons (or strategies, or plans, or counterclaims, or defenses) in the world are useless without the courage to use them.

Epilogue

One Regret

Researching this work, I read a lengthy article written by a San Diego doctor (using the *nom de plume* Dr. Marian Joyce), which chronicled her experience being sued for medical malpractice.[34] Her story changed entirely how I look at clients. As a client herself, she describes her feelings and worries in gripping and honest detail. In particular, she describes her fear and helplessness understanding the legal process and her interaction with the insurance defense attorney hired to represent her.

> *My insurance company assigned me an attorney before the lawsuit was even filed in order to intercept the badgering correspondence. My attorney arranged to come to my office to meet me in person, dressed very casually in jeans and cowboy boots. It was Friday, but his attire did not inspire confidence. He did not seem concerned, which worried me immensely. Perhaps he was trying to set me at ease, but his nonchalant approach was far from reassuring to me.*

---

[34] *Paradise Lost: When Clients Commit Suicide*, by Dr. n Joyce, psychotherapy.net, 2013

We have treated our clients in exactly the same way. Casual attire, casual attitude. "Don't worry, we have you covered. That's a trivial issue. Don't worry. Not a problem; just be patient." We behaved that way thinking, as the doctor suspected of the attorney, that projecting an image of calm confidence would be reassuring.

"Do you want to go over the details of the case?" I asked.

Why did I feel like the only one ready to work? Don't you see the danger I am in, I thought. Don't you understand what is at stake?

Once again, his cavalier approach was not reassuring...I thought of my dentist, needle poised over my gaping mouth: "This won't hurt a bit."[35]

As with the doctor, the clients may have interpreted our actions as, "We don't care that much about you. You're just another client. Your case is nothing special." If a client broke down in tears in a meeting or on the phone, we would still project calm confidence and tell them that everything was under control. They didn't need that.

They needed to know about the sleepless nights analyzing and re-analyzing their case. *Did we miss something? Did we pursue that angle? What if we don't have all the facts? Are we making an incorrect assumption? Why did the bank do that? Have we been thinking about this case all wrong?* I wouldn't reveal these all-nighters because I feared if the client knew how much time we spent analyzing and re-analyzing the case, they would think we lacked confidence in our strategy.

But for many, they would have felt better. Many would be reassured that we were doing everything in our power to protect them, and that we were personally invested in achieving the best result for them. They could be confident that we will not be outworked or out-thought.

You are not alone. Don't be scared and don't feel hopeless. We will never,

---

[35] "Dr. Joyce" gets it eventually, but she figured it out on her own. *"By then, six months into my dealings with the legal world, I was beginning to understand that the lawsuit was solely about money, how much the plaintiff's attorney could get for her clients, how little the insurance company could pay on my behalf. "My attorney" was really working for the liability insurance company, not for me."*

ever, give up. Even if all of our efforts fail, we will have you prepared to recover and climb out. However, we never had case conclude with the client out of money and filing for bankruptcy. If you understand the method and philosophy, then you understand it will *never* happen.

Author's Note

As noted in the introduction, all of the events described in the foregoing work are true. However, with respect to clients, my and/or my consulting firm's involvement was subject to confidentiality restrictions. Therefore, to protect client confidentiality, we did not include the names of the clients, obviously, and refrained from mentioning the specific name of any party to the case.

Moreover, in an effort to conceal client identities further, many non-material facts in the cases were changed. For example, a person described as a man in his thirties with a $2 million loan on an apartment building in Smyrna, Ga., might be described as a woman with a $1.8 million loan on a shopping center in Charlotte, unless those particular facts were relevant to the situation, process or outcome in the case.

"Maria" and "Gary" are real people (as is "Randolph Everett"), and their story is true, but their names are changed for privacy.

All research and references contained in the foregoing work are accurate and true to the best knowledge of the author but have not been independently verified. It was on the Internet, so it must be true. Any corrections, questions, or attorney cease-and-desist letters will be cheerfully received by the author and promptly addressed as necessary.

The author makes no representations as to accuracy, completeness, suitability, or validity of any information herein and assumes no liability for any errors, omissions, losses, injuries, or damages arising from reliance on its contents. And seriously, what's the potential upside of threatening legal action against a person whose area of expertise is protecting people and their money from creditors and lawyers? Just a thought. Instead, send me an e-mail, or pick up the phone and call. I'll make the correction or answer your questions, as applicable. We don't want any trouble.

The opinions expressed herein are solely those of the author on the date of publication and do not reflect the opinions any current or former business associates or clients of the author, virtually any banker or loan asset manager you could find, Sun Tzu, the month of May, any living breathing human being on the planet in certain instances, and certainly no lawyers.

Thank you for your support.

Acknowledgments

My son Griffin will graduate from high school next year, and upon my telling him I wrote this, responded, "Who is your target audience?" Oh my. Griffin, I have told you that I hope you have many accomplishments in your life, but all that matters to me is your honesty and character and the kind of man you become. You will understand why when you finish reading this book. By Thursday. And, yes, there will be a quiz.

My toddler son, David, will enjoy building a fort using the book and tossing the book from high places and/or into the bathtub, which I will treasure even with the Kindle version.

My wife, Elizabeth, is what Rudyard Kipling meant when he said, "The silliest woman can manage a clever man, but it takes a clever woman to manage a fool." Thank you for your astounding patience, support, and guile.

My Dad is the most honest and genuine man I've ever known, and I wish I inherited the ease at which he can laugh at himself. I am grateful for my mother's love, and particularly what she taught me about professionalism and being precise in one's communication.

My editor, Melissa Heffner, is a delightful and thorough young lady. Passive Voice trembles at her approach. I am also grateful for the creativity, patience, and awesome name of cover artist Ida Fia Sveningsson.

My producer, Melissa Smith, is almost unbearably focused. She accomplished with ruthless efficiency the two most critical tasks of the project: 1) Call me at least daily and find out what I'm doing, and 2) Tell me to *stop doing that* and do what I'm *supposed* to be doing. My gratitude knows no bounds.

My dear friend Melissa van Rossum gave me the confidence to write. Rather, Melissa gave me the confidence to publish what I have written, by way of espresso, conversations on philosophy and human nature, and paranormal fiction, whatever *that* is. A Mastermind indeed. Good lookin', too.

I also appreciate Jim Yost for his incessant and sometimes irritating optimism, and Caroline Massey Yost, who edited many of the original versions of the case study material.

15 years ago, Deborah Goodman told me she thought I "write beautifully," and she wasn't just being nice. I can't say I would have attempted this absent Deborah's small, thoughtful, and unsolicited compliment.

Most of all, I appreciate Maria for telling her story, and the example she sets by showing up every day for life, working hard, and moving on. Thank you for making this happen. Insisting, actually.

About the Author

After graduating with honors from the University of Georgia School of Law, Clay Westbrook moved to Atlanta with a car load of belongings, a Labrador Retriever, and dreams of wealth and success. After the real world swiftly crushed those dreams, he spent 15 years practicing corporate transactions and real estate law, working with, and learning from, many of the most talented and/or insufferable lawyers this country has ever produced.

Clay and the practice of law parted ways for good in 2009. The breakup was amicable, with both Clay and the legal profession drastically improved as a result. Clay now works in corporate finance and financial restructuring and was actively involved in settling over $450 million in problem loans for clients across the country. He also developed expertise in negotiating business breakups, litigation and bankruptcy strategy consulting, and settling accounts with taxing authorities and disputes with governmental entities.

His consulting firm, Ascent, helps business owners, attorneys, CPAs and other professionals, providing seminars, training, and consulting on negotiation, litigation, bankruptcy, and dispute resolution. He most enjoys helping people in complicated situations that require original thought, and working with talented professionals who wish to better serve their clients.

Clay also enjoys writing, history, sports, and the outdoors. Ideally, he would hike in the mountains all day, and then stay in a nice hotel. He resides in Atlanta with his wife, two sons, and two cats with whom he maintains a fragile truce.